Creative
PROGRAMMING IDEAS
FOR JUNIOR HIGH MINISTRY

ZONDERVAN/YOUTH SPECIALTIES BOOKS

Professional Resources
Called to Care
Developing Student Leaders
Feeding Your Forgotten Soul
Growing Up in America
High School Ministry
How to Recruit and Train Volunteer
    Youth Workers (Previously released as
    Unsung Heroes)
Junior High Ministry
The Ministry of Nurture
Organizing Your Youth Ministry
The Youth Minister's Survival Guide
Youth Ministry Nuts and Bolts

Discussion Starter Resources
Amazing Tension Getters
Get 'Em Talking
High School TalkSheets
Hot Talks
Junior High TalkSheets
Option Plays
Tension Getters
Tension Getters Two

Special Needs and Issues
The Complete Student Missions
    Handbook
Divorce Recovery for Teenagers
Ideas for Social Action
Intensive Care: Helping Teenagers in
    Crisis
Rock Talk
Teaching the Truth About Sex
Up Close and Personal: How to Build
    Community in Your Youth Group

Youth Ministry Programming
Adventure Games
Creative Programming Ideas for Junior
    High Ministry
Creative Socials and Special Events
Good Clean Fun
Good Clean Fun, Volume 2
Great Games for City Kids
Great Ideas for Small Youth Groups

Greatest Skits on Earth
Greatest Skits on Earth, Volume 2
Holiday Ideas for Youth Groups (Revised
    Edition)
Junior High Game Nights
On-Site: 40 On-Location Youth Programs
Play It! Great Games for Groups
Super Sketches for Youth Ministry
Teaching the Bible Creatively
The Youth Specialties Handbook for
    Great Camps and Retreats

4th-6th Grade Ministry
Attention Grabbers for 4th-6th Graders
Great Games for 4th-6th Graders
How to Survive Middle School
Incredible Stories
More Attention Grabbers for 4th-6th
    Graders
More Great Games for 4th-6th Graders
More Quick and Easy Activities for 4th-
    6th Graders
Quick and Easy Activities for 4th-6th
    Graders

Clip Art
ArtSource™ Volume 1—Fantastic
    Activities
ArtSource™ Volume 2—Borders,
    Symbols, Holidays, and Attention
    Getters
ArtSource™ Volume 3—Sports
ArtSource™ Volume 4—Phrases and
    Verses
ArtSource™ Volume 5—Amazing
    Oddities and Appalling Images
ArtSource™ Volume 6—Spiritual Topics
Youth Specialties Clip Art Book
Youth Specialties Clip Art Book, Volume 2

**OTHER BOOKS BY
DARRELL PEARSON**

Parents as Partners in Youth Ministry
    (Scripture Press/Victor)

Creative
PROGRAMMING IDEAS
for JUNIOR HIGH MINISTRY

Dozens of Easy-to-Use Ideas for Youth Meetings,
Sunday School, Camps and Retreats, Music and Drama,
Recreation, and Much More

Steve Dickie and
Darrell Pearson

ZondervanPublishingHouse
A Division of HarperCollinsPublishers

Creative Programming Ideas for Junior High Ministry

Copyright © 1992 by Youth Specialties, Inc.

Youth Specialties Books, 1224 Greenfield Drive, El Cajon,
   California 92021, are published by Zondervan Publishing House,
   1415 Lake Drive, S.E., Grand Rapids, Michigan 49506

Library of Congress Cataloging-in-Publication Data

Dickie, Steve, 1956-
      Creative programming ideas for junior high ministry / Steve
Dickie, Darrell Pearson.
                p.   cm.
      Subtitle: Dozens of easy-to-use ideas for youth meetings, Sunday
school, camps and retreats, music and drama, recreation, and much more.
      ISBN 0-310-54151-4
      1. Church work with teenagers. I. Pearson, Darrell, 1954-
II. Title.
BV4447.D48 1992
259'.23—dc20   91-27065
                                                      CIP

Edited by Lory Floyd and Elizabeth Abbott
Design and typography by Rogers Design and Associates
Cover photography by Mark Rayburn and Jack Rogers

Printed in the United States of America

92 93 94 95 96 97 98 99 / ML / 10 9 8 7 6 5 4 3 2 1

About the YouthSource™ Publishing Group

YouthSource™ books, tapes, videos, and other resources pool the expertise of three of the finest youth ministry resource providers in the world:

• **Campus Life Books**—publishers of the award-winning *Campus Life* magazine, who for nearly fifty years have helped high schoolers live Christian lives.

• **Youth Specialties**—serving ministers to middle school, junior high, and high school youth for over twenty years through books, magazines, and training events such as the National Youth Workers Convention.

• **Zondervan Publishing House**—one of the oldest, largest, and most respected evangelical Christian publishers in the world.

Campus Life	Youth Specialties	Zondervan
465 Gundersen Dr.	1224 Greenfield Dr.	1415 Lake Dr. S.E.
Carol Stream, IL 60188	El Cajon, CA 92021	Grand Rapids, MI 49506
708/260-6200	619/440-2333	616/698-6900

Contents

Foreword

Junior high ministry is the most important ministry in the church.

Yeah, sure, I know that there are lots of other ministries in the church that are very, very important . . . and I know that people who make blanket statements like the one above are arrogant snobs . . . and I also know that it is impossible for me to be objective because I do a lot of speaking and writing about junior high ministry.

Still . . . junior high ministry is the most important ministry in the church.

Think about it. Where else do you have the opportunity to influence young adults (yes, junior highers *are* young adults) *before* they make the big decisions of their lives?

You certainly can't wait until they reach high school. In today's accelerated culture, high school ministry is basically rehabilitation. Many, if not most, high school students have already decided whether to have sex or not, whether to take drugs or not, whether to drink alcohol or not, whether to give God a place in their lives or not. Forty years ago, decisions like those were made in college. Twenty years ago, they were made in high school. Now they are being made in junior high school, sometimes even earlier.

That's why I believe junior high ministry is so important. Early adolescence—the junior high years—is an especially critical time in the human life span and therefore an especially critical time for ministry.

But every ministry of the church is important. From the senior pastor to the janitor, Scripture teaches that the body of Christ is made up of many parts, all of them making the body complete. Yet Scripture does encourage us to "treat with special honor" those parts that are often thought of as "less honorable" (1 Corinthians 12:23).

Maybe it's time to give special honor to people like Darrell Pearson and Steve Dickie, who have given the best years of their lives to make a difference with junior highers. Junior high workers rarely get special honor. Instead, they get low pay supplemented with a good deal of sympathy. Sometimes all they get is derision and ridicule. That's why it's hard to find junior high workers who have kept at it for more than two or three years.

Steve and Darrell have kept at it for a combined total of twenty-seven years. They have proven that the phrase "professional junior high minister" is not an oxymoron. Over the long haul, both of these men have remained faithful to the calling of junior high ministry and they have brought a degree of professionalism to it that is extremely rare.

Like I said, I do a lot of speaking and writing about junior high ministry. And while I have been out speaking and writing about junior high ministry, Darrell and Steve have been out *doing* it. They have been in the trenches, trying out the old ideas and coming up with new ones to meet the needs of junior high kids. They have quietly established themselves as two of the most experienced and creative junior high workers in the country.

This book is so valuable because it is not based on theory; it is not another book on the theology or philosophy of junior high ministry. Instead, Darrell Pearson and Steve Dickie have provided us with a practical sourcebook of tried-and-tested ideas written especially for junior high workers. No longer will you be forced to adapt material written for older youths or to spend long hours trying to invent your own. This book contains everything you need: the nuts and bolts of junior high ministry, creative programs, ideas and activities that work with junior high kids, and tips on how to use them with success.

It's time to give special honor to people who work with junior highers in the church. I can think of no better way than to provide them with a copy of this excellent book.

—*WAYNE RICE*

Acknowledgments

To all those who taught us to think creatively, allowed us to experiment unconditionally, were patient with our failures, encouraging in our successes, and willing to try just about any outrageous idea that our devious little minds came up with—even when they were dumb, silly, or booooooorrrrrrrring!

A special word of thanks to our friends at Youth Specialties for the opportunity to write this thing: Noel Becchetti for wisdom and guidance, Leslie Lutes for patience, and Kathi George for correcting those pesky dangling participles!

Thanks to James and Martha Dickie (Dad and Mom) for being proud of me and my decisions (I was your ultimate creative idea!); and to Lori Dickie and Kristine Jones (sisters) for putting up with all my creative antics during our early years.

Thanks to Stacey Wedgbury (my trusted administrative assistant and friend) for your incredible typing, amazing spelling, and awesome laugh.

Thanks to my mentors for doing things well and giving me the opportunity to watch, come alongside, and then lead.

Thanks to the staff and students of Garden Grove Community Church, Garden Grove, California, and South Coast Community Church, Irvine, California (my first two churches), for allowing me to experiment, learn the ropes, fail gracefully, and occasionally succeed triumphantly.

Thanks to the staff, students, and parents of Bel Air Presbyterian Church, Los Angeles, California (my current church), for encouraging me, supporting me, praying for me, and always asking me if I had finished this project yet. Yeah!
—*STEVE DICKIE*

My special thanks to my great interns —Arleigh Gibson, Alan Guffey, Mark Nichols, Rick Chase, Steve Morgan, Keith Robinson, Lindsay Case, Dave Turner, Beth Roome, James Holsworth, Mark Epperson, and Katie Armstrong—whose brilliant ideas made me look like a programming genius.

I'd also like to thank my parents, Will and Eileen, for their lifelong modeling of church commitment that taught me long-term ministry; First Presbyterian Church of Colorado Springs, which graciously has allowed me a place to do that ministry; and Rose, for endless FAX and phone calls that, unfortunately, are also a part of ministry.
—*DARRELL PEARSON*

Introduction

Outside of Steve's office window is an incredible sight—an enormous framework of a building that will, hopefully, end up being a church someday. It doesn't look much like a church yet; it's simply beam after beam of supporting structures that will hold in place all the materials that will make it a place where ministry can happen.

This book is not a quick fix to junior high ministry problems. It is not stuffed with every conceivable program idea to give you something to use with your students every day of the next year. Rather, it's a structure, a framework, an overall support that is designed to give you the necessary beams to hang your own program on. Our programs don't look alike, and yours should not look like ours. Each junior high ministry needs to have an identity all its own, an identity special to the students and adults who are a part of it. We have stuffed this book with ideas not so that you can copy what we have done, but so that you can use them to create a program all your own. We hope the book helps your ministry!

—STEVE DICKIE and DARRELL PEARSON

SECTION ONE:
SETTING THE STAGE–PULLING YOUR PROGRAM TOGETHER

CHAPTER ONE

UNDERSTANDING THE NEEDS OF JUNIOR HIGHERS

By Steve Dickie

I must admit that in my early days of junior high ministry I made a few mistakes. Okay, I made more than a few, but none was larger than my failure to keep program in perspective. You see, I was a program junkie. I would spend hours upon hours creating incredible programs that would surely be etched in the Junior High Ministry Hall of Fame. Once the programs were in place, I would sit back and marvel at my awesome creations. You would have been impressed—bicycle rodeos, amazing theme nights, Christian rock concerts, movie extravaganzas, scavenger hunts, incredible camps and retreats, beach bonfires, sports programs, and some pretty hot Bible studies. Great programs, but with one major problem—my junior highers didn't always come. All the right ingredients were there, but I had forgotten one major component: I had failed to examine the needs of my kids; I was often aiming at the wrong target.

Creating programs without understanding needs can be compared to hunting rabbits by standing at the edge of a forest and randomly unloading a shotgun in all directions. Not smart. We may happen to hit something eventually, but we are probably missing the real target entirely. We must first discover our target before we attempt to fire. Our challenge is simple. If we want our programs to be effective, we must first examine the needs of our kids. Programs emerge out of needs, not the other way around. Our creative efforts are wasted if we miss this mark.

FOCUS OF CREATIVE PROGRAMMING

1. Understand Needs - - ▸ 2. Establish Goals - - ▸ 3. Create Program

◂——— C R E A T I V I T Y ———▸

(The Rope That Ties It All Together)

The good news is that you *can* do it. Whether you are twenty-two or fifty-six, thirty-four or seventy-five, you can understand junior high kids. They *want* to be understood!

Although understanding junior highers can be an enjoyable task, it can also require a lot of work. There's really no quick fix. You have to put in the time to do it. I was reminded of this principle ever so painfully (to my batting average, that is) during this year's softball season. For the past couple of years, I've played on a club team in West Los Angeles. After a two-month break following our summer league, I really struggled when we started our fall schedule. I tried every possible remedy to reverse my slide. I bought new batting gloves, borrowed a heavier bat, wore a different hat, adjusted my stance, blamed the pitches, blamed my cleats, and blamed the quality of my bubble gum. I even blamed my wife for washing my pants wrong. The problem, however, turned out to be me. I hadn't bothered to practice. I expected to go right out there and hit dingers without putting in the time. If we want to be good at what we do, whether it's softball or working with junior highers, we have to put in the work. There's no other way. If we are willing to do our homework, understanding junior highers can happen—successfully!

OPEN YOUR EYES TO THE JUNIOR HIGH WORLD

When you open your eyes to the junior high world, you may be amazed at what you see. Did you know that thirteen-year-olds can sing *The Brady Bunch* theme song and burp simultaneously, speak without breathing for four continuous

hours, personally drive up AT&T stock with one week's phone calls, fill three toilet bowls with one can of shaving cream, drink orange juice through the nostrils, and memorize 100 years of baseball statistics—yet still forget yesterday's homework assignment? While you certainly will discover some pretty bizarre things when you look into the junior high world, you will also learn of some disturbing things. Did you know that

- One out of every three eighth graders has tried an illicit drug?
- One out of every four eighth graders has used alcohol twenty or more times?
- Fifteen percent of seventh graders and 18 percent of eighth graders will have sexual intercourse one or more times this year?[1]

Yes, junior highers are wild and crazy, but they also face great pressures. That's why they need people like you so much. As you open your eyes to who they are and what they are like, you will see and hear things that you never knew existed and rediscover realities that you may have long forgotten. Some kids will amaze you, others may startle you, but with hope, all will motivate you to minister to them. Let's start this journey by taking a look at two important areas—universal needs and local needs.

UNIVERSAL NEEDS. These needs are basically universal to all junior high kids. Developmentally, junior high-age people are similar physically, mentally, socially, and spiritually. Chances are that a junior higher in Tustin, California, will have similar universal needs as a junior higher in Hampton, Iowa.

I was able to get a good look at this principle when Darrell and I were leaders of "On the Edge," a national junior high event sponsored by Youth Specialties. As we traveled around the country, I was amazed at the similarities among kids from region to region. I remember telling one great group from the South that if I could somehow "beam" them (that's *Star Trek* talk) into my California group, the differences (besides their accents) would hardly be noticeable. In light of this, we can trust most research on early adolescent trends, since junior highers' developmental needs are universal. Here is a great chart[2] to help you understand the universal needs of a typical junior higher.

THE JUNIOR HIGHER

Physical

Preadolescent
—Sexual maturation and rapid physical growth
—Coordination development increases

Early Adolescent
—Period of rapid physical growth and sexual maturation
—Changes in voice and sex-related characteristics

NEEDS: Acceptance of looks; knowledge about caring for their bodies; answers regarding their changing bodies (sex).

Social

Preadolescent
—Vacillation between periods of friendship and isolation
—Social dependence continues

Early Adolescent
—Peer group focus
—Weakening ties with families
—Emerging social independence

NEEDS: Feeling group acceptance; healthy times with the opposite sex; individualism in the face of peer pressure; concern for others.

Intellectual

Preadolescent
—Complete generality of thought
—Spurts of abstraction

Early Adolescent
—Ability to deal with hypothetical issues
—Propositional thinking
—Formal reasoning begins

NEEDS: Understanding, acceptance, and encouragement; reinforcement of positive attitudes; self-discipline; role models; reasons for doing things.

Moral and Spiritual

Preadolescent
—Other-awareness emerges
—Parental values present
—Legalistic black-and-white thinking

Early Adolescent
—Development of strong idealism
—Questioning of previous values
—Spiritual inquisitiveness

NEEDS: Understanding that Jesus and the Bible are applicable to their lives; answers to valid questions; truth based on fact over feelings; understanding of basics.

LOCAL NEEDS. Although universal

needs are usually static, local needs can vary considerably. I learned this truth when I took a new church position in West Los Angeles after spending seven years in Orange County, California. Although my new church was only a commuter drive up the freeway, I soon discovered the "distance" between the two local cultures was great. My O.C. kids surfed, my L.A. kids pretended they did; my O.C. kids liked pop dance music, my L.A. kids liked heavy metal; and my O.C. kids came from primarily white neighborhoods, while my L.A. kids came from racially mixed communities. Although they were all very "Southern California" junior high kids, the two groups were very different in clothing, hairstyles, fads, music, expressions, slang, and interests. The most creative programs miss the mark if they are not meeting the needs of the community you live in.

I recall seeing this happen during my college years when I was a leader in an incredibly successful high school ministry. People from all over the country would visit our program and attempt to duplicate it in their home communities. Most failed. They were impressed with our visible program (the technology, flash, and large numbers), but they failed to see the long hours, countless strategy meetings, and great pains that were taken to make it fresh, relevant, and effective in meeting local needs. Gather and borrow ideas, observe other groups, and implement someone else's successes, but be careful of copying the hot program across town or the one featured in the latest youth magazine without making sure it fits *your* needs.

STUDY THE JUNIOR HIGH WORLD

As I shared earlier, discovering needs takes work—you must study. Here are a few ways to start.

TWENTY CREATIVE WAYS TO RESEARCH THE NEEDS OF THE JUNIOR HIGH WORLD

1. Have a kid give you a tour of a music store, a school, an arcade, or some other junior high haunt.
2. Pass out a survey at a local hangout.
3. Volunteer to chaperon a dance at a local school.
4. Coach a junior high level sports team.
5. Use a video camera or a tape recorder to interview kids.
6. Participate in the police ride-along program.
7. Tape junk food to your shirt and dash into a room of seventh graders.
8. Attend (or join) the local P.T.A.
9. Join the school booster club.
10. Attend school events (sports, dramas, concerts).
11. Throw rocks at kids—note the cultural language responses.
12. Subscribe to local school papers.
13. Employ a junior higher to mow your lawn.
14. Stand near a local hangout dressed like a rock star—offer to sign autographs.
15. Attend school board meetings.
16. Buy a jet ski and hang out at a beach, a lake, or a river.
17. Go to an arcade—challenge kids to video games.
18. Organize pickup basketball, football, and other games at the local park.

19. Sit in a mall and watch people.
20. Cram peanut butter into your ears, walk up to junior highers, and tell them your brain is leaking—note their reactions.

Looking for a few more practical ideas? Here are some of the steps that I have taken in my study of junior high needs.

READ. I will read just about anything: cereal boxes, soup cans, and even shampoo bottles. You name it, I'll read it. Outside of my latest copy of *Sports Illustrated*, there is nothing like a good box of cookies (the box, not the cookies). I especially like attacking material on early adolescence.

When I first began my work in junior high ministry, I spent considerable time at the local library reading all the adolescent development texts. These books gave me a good handle on understanding the universal needs of kids.

I also discovered the Christian bookstore and the many fine resources that were available to me. I spend hours at my favorite store gathering ideas and looking for great talk topics and titles. As a matter of fact, I even buy something every once in a while, which is why the owners let me hang out for so long. You might try having your church purchase the material for its library. The church pays for it, but you get to use it.

I encourage you to read *Junior High Ministry* by Wayne Rice.[3] I devoured the copy of this classic book that was given to me during my first day of full-time junior high ministry. Much of what I now know about junior high work can be traced back to what I learned from that book. Now in a revised edition, it is still a "must read" for anyone working with early adolescents.

You should also check out a few good magazines. Three of my favorite Christian ones are *Breakaway*, for junior high boys, *Brio*, for junior high girls (Focus on the Family Ministries), and *Campus Life*. Although *Campus Life* is written with high school students in mind, it is still relevant to junior highers. You would also be wise to read the current issues of secular music and teen fashion magazines. Try checking out *Sassy, Seventeen*, or the countless music mags that can be found on most racks. These help us keep up with the latest youth trends. (Actually, I learn more from the advertisements than the articles.)

Don't forget to take advantage of the newspaper as a study source of trends and needs. Frankly, I think the daily reading of a newspaper should be required of every youth worker. If you live in a small town, you might want to consider subscribing to a national edition paper (*New York Times, Washington Post*) or a news magazine (*Time, Newsweek*). When it comes to researching needs, I also highly recommend anything published by the Barna Research Group.[4] Check out *The Frog in the Kettle: What Christians Need to Know About Life in the Year 2000* by George Barna.[5] Finally, a subscription to *Youthworker Update*,[6] available from Youth Specialties, is a wise move. Full of all sorts of trends, issues, and odds and ends, this newsletter would be a good addition to your library.

LISTEN AND WATCH. Another excellent means of understanding junior highers is to study their music. When I realized a number of years ago that I had lost track of the music culture, I asked Eddie, a seventh grade music expert, to give me a tour of a local record store. He walked me through the top hits and explained the types of audiences that followed each group. He also introduced me to some of the music magazines where I could keep up on what's hot and what's not. I now make a record store tour a regular event. Kids love showing me around their music world. You might want to make a habit of checking out the back page of *Rolling Stone* magazine that lists the current top hits.

As you know, *listening* to music is only half of the modern experience. You can *watch* it, too. Spend some time watching the television video channels. An evening of MTV will put you in touch with the latest fashion statements, slang phrases, and dance styles. It will also sober you regarding the need kids have for a relationship with Christ. Once again, pay close attention to the commercials; you will learn a lot about adolescent culture by seeing what Madison Avenue is targeting.

PICK A BRAIN. One of the best ways to study the junior high world is to ask questions of people who ought to know about it.

First, glean information from other youth workers. Not only can they provide valuable insight into the local culture, they can also become a means of support for your efforts.

Second, meet with local school principals and teachers. You can learn much from these people and you can also gain some important contacts to use later in your ministry. Try subscribing to the school newspaper. At the end of the school year, send notes to local junior high principals, thanking them for their work. Sure, it's a PR move, but it also communicates that you value them.

Third, pick the brains of professional

counselors in the area. During the first month of one of my church positions, my supervisor set up an appointment for me to meet a local psychologist who specialized in adolescence. He became an important source of information, encouragement, and reference when I got stuck or felt in over my head.

Take a moment and list a few people you can contact and whose brains you can pick.
• Area youth workers_____
• School staff members: _____
• Counselors: _____
• Others: _____

Not too sure what to talk about? Try asking these questions as a place to start.

• Describe a typical junior higher in the community.
• What are the pressures local junior highers face?
• How are local junior highers different than they were five years ago?
• Where do local junior highers hang out?
• What does it take to meet the needs of local junior highers?

SURVEY. There is nothing like a good survey to research needs. When you invite kids to share their opinions, you not only gain insight into their likes but their dislikes as well. This is a great way to learn where or where not to target your creative programming.

I've discovered that most junior high kids like to answer surveys. Not only do they enjoy the process of filling out the form, they also love any opportunity to express their opinions. When you think about it, who ever asks junior highers what they think? While we gather vital information, we also communicate a powerful message to them—they are significant and their opinions are valued!

Whom do you survey? The possibilities are endless. Once you survey your junior highers, try surveying parents, school administrators, teachers, church staff members, professional counselors, music shop owners, and so on.

What do you ask in a survey? Simply ask what you want to know. You might focus on getting a general feel for the local junior high culture, or you could gather information on specific issues.

What insights or information would you like to know about your junior highers? List below.

_____
_____
_____
_____
_____

The following is a sample survey that you can use with your junior highers, or you might want to create your own to gather information about the issues you just listed.

SURVEY:
TELL US ABOUT THE
JUNIOR HIGH WORLD

What's the best part about being junior high age?

What's the worst part about being junior high age?

Help us understand what's hot and what's not in the junior high world. Share with us what is popular in each of these categories.

1. Music groups
2. TV shows
3. Clothing styles
4. Hairstyles
5. Fads
6. Sayings and expressions
7. Hangouts
8. Dance styles
9. Vices (drugs, alcohol, stealing, and so on)
10. Heroes

We're interested in what you think about these topics. Share your feelings with us.

1. Heaven
2. Parents
3. Country
4. Friends
5. Sex
6. Future
7. Marriage and divorce
8. School
9. Rules
10. Fears

Finally, complete these two sentences.

1. When I look in the mirror, I see . . .

2. When I think of God, I think of . . .

SPEND TIME IN
THE JUNIOR HIGH WORLD

One of the major errors we youth workers make (rookies and veterans alike) is that we often fail to spend time with kids. It is easy to get so involved with building our creative programs that we forget to do what matters most—be with the kids. If we want to discover their needs, we have to enter into their world.

Jesus himself was our example in this regard. He spent time with his people and he never ministered from a distance. When you think about it, the incarnation—God entering the world as a human—is a wonderful model for youth ministry.

THE FEAR FACTOR. I believe one of the major reasons we fail to spend time with junior highers is that entering into their world is scary. Although we may fear not knowing what to talk about or what to do with them, our greatest fear is that we won't be liked.

Bob, a retired gentleman who volunteers on our student ministries board, had an interesting experience in this area. During one of our committee meetings, I challenged the members of our board to visit our student programs. I told them if they wanted to best serve and support our staff, they needed to spend time with our kids firsthand. Bob showed up the next Sunday morning. Expecting to sit in the back and observe, Bob was surprised when I asked him to take charge of a small group of seventh graders during a discussion time. He jumped right in, circled his kids, and went at it. Afterward, he was ecstatic. Not only had his group listened well and shared freely, they also seemed to really like him. A few days later, one of the kids who was in his group approached me. "I hope Bob comes back," he said. "I really think he liked us." Amazing? Not really. Junior high kids are afraid that they won't be liked, too. Show them you like them and you'll probably win.

What are some of the fears you have about spending time with junior highers?

_____

_____

_____

What are some practical steps you can take to overcome those fears?

_____

_____

_____

"WHERE DO I GO?" If we want to understand the needs of junior highers, we need to go into their world. Jim Rayburn, a young minister in the 1930s, put this principle into action. Frustrated with the outdated and ineffective means of reaching teenagers for Christ, Rayburn began going to the students at their high schools rather than requiring them to come to the church building. His vision resulted in the creation of Young Life, an organization committed to "going where kids congregate and accepting them as they are."

When I was in college, coaching a junior high basketball team for the city parks department, I decided to put this principle into action. Every Saturday morning we always found ourselves short a player or two. To avoid the forfeit, I would drive over to the local convenience store and recruit a couple of junior highers (tall ones, of course) to play. Through that experience, I soon learned where junior high kids hung out in my community. (I also created a very good basketball team.)

Where do junior high kids in your community congregate?

_____

_____

_____

"WHAT DO I SAY?" Before saying

anything, it is sometimes best just to watch. One of the best places for junior high watching in our town is a shopping center with a central courtyard lined with various shops—surf wear, cards and gifts, sporting goods, ice cream, and a movie theater. One evening, as my wife and I waited for a movie over ice cream cones, I watched and listened. By simply observing what was in front of me, I learned quite a bit about the junior high world.

After watching for a while, it's also important to talk with the kids. Some of the greatest conversations I have with kids are at the mall, in the grocery checkout line, at the video store, or at the hamburger joint. I like to start conversations by asking questions about things kids are into—music, sports, television, movies, or styles. This usually paves the way for us to enter into deeper conversation. Or maybe we should do what one youth worker friend of mine does. He just tackles kids and wrestles them to the ground.

When I talk to kids, it is important for me to keep track of what they tell me. When they communicate something of significance, I write it down.

REMEMBER YOUR OWN JUNIOR HIGH WORLD

I am convinced that remembering the past is a valuable way of understanding the present. Although we cannot return to those thrilling, sometimes chilling, days of yesteryear, we can still attempt to recall the myriad emotions, dreams, fears, and pains that confront junior highers every morning. We cannot confuse the "way we did it" and "when we were in junior high" with the needs of today's kids. We can, however, keep our

personal experiences before us to help us minister with understanding and compassion.

I love to get in touch with my junior high years. I can still spend hours at my parents' house rummaging through a box I keep in the corner of an upstairs closet. My mom calls it "Steve's box," and my dad calls it "that pile of junk." I call it my contact with the past. The box is filled with priceless memories—a rare "A" on a math test, pencil drawings of dragsters and fighter planes, letters from old crushes, a rock and fossil collection, tattered Al Kaline and Ernie Banks baseball cards, science fair project notes, and even my original seventh grade P.E. uniform. I can pore over this stuff for hours. If you don't have your own box of memories, here are some great steps you can take to learn the needs of junior highers today by remembering the past.

WRITE AN AUTOBIOGRAPHY. When I first started working with junior highers, I wrote an autobiography of my junior high years. It was amazing to me how many dissimilar and unconnected episodes began to actually fit together like a giant puzzle. It took the passage of many years for me to see that God was very much at work in me, molding and shaping me into the person I was to become. The process can't help but make us better "sensitive-to-needs" youth leaders.

VISIT YOUR ROOTS. A few years ago, I flew into Indianapolis, Indiana—my hometown during my elementary and junior high school years. With video camera and tape recorder in hand, I set out to get in touch with my past. I talked to girls (now women) who used to babysit me. The owners of my boyhood home let me poke around my old bedroom. I even found the tree where I had carved my name next to some young flame. As my wife and I wandered around my boyhood street corners, favorite trees, and baseball fields, I narrated many stories tied to each spot. I came home with an incredible supply of new illustrations to use for talks.

Visiting my old school was a powerful experience. As I walked around the building and grounds, I actually began to feel long forgotten emotions—the pain of rejection by a girl I liked, the confusion of trying to cope with my self-worth and confidence, and the pressure of wanting to be accepted. I had tears in my eyes. Now when I look into the eyes of a fearful junior high kid, I look with a deeper, enlightened sense of compassion—I remember.

STAY IN TOUCH WITH THE JUNIOR HIGH WORLD

In my workouts, I've learned that staying in shape is often more difficult than getting in shape. The same principle applies to meeting the needs of young people. Youth workers must continually make sure they are aiming their efforts at the right targets. We cannot lose touch with the junior high world and later discover that the targets we've been aiming at have moved. The need to reevaluate applies to both rookies and veterans alike. It is our task to make sure the hot programs of today don't become the ineffective programs of tomorrow.

Evaluation is important for this simple reason: Junior high kids are worth it. Any attempt to understand their needs begins and ends with this fact. The passage of Matthew 9:35–38, in which Jesus exhorts his disciples to meet needs, reminds me of this fact.

Jesus went through all the towns and villages, teaching in their synagogues, preaching the good news of the kingdom and healing every disease and sickness. When he saw the crowds, he had compassion on them, because they were harassed and helpless, like sheep without a shepherd. Then he said to his disciples, "The harvest is plentiful but the workers are few. Ask the Lord of the harvest, therefore, to send out workers into his harvest field."

Junior high kids need you. Your efforts to understand them and to build creative programs to meet their needs are important and worthy tasks. You are now on the road and heading in the right direction. On the next stop, Darrell will help you set the direction for your programs by developing goals. These goals will meet the needs that you are now discovering. Go for it. We believe in you!

ENDNOTES

1. Data are from a study by Search Institute (Minneapolis) of students in Colorado and Minnesota. Quoted in David R. Veerman, *Reaching Kids Before High School* (Wheaton, Ill.: Victor, 1990), 20–21.
2. Earl D. Wilson, *You Try Being a Teenager* (Portland, Ore.: Multnomah Press, 1982). The chart is adapted from Figure 1, p. 23; the added notes on needs are my own.
3. Wayne Rice, *Junior High Ministry* (Grand Rapids: YS/Zondervan, 1987).
4. Barna Research Group, P.O. Box 4152, Glendale, CA 91222-0152.

5. George Barna, *The Frog in the Kettle: What Christians Need to Know About Life in the Year 2000* (Ventura, Calif.: Regal, 1990).

6. *Youthworker Update*, Youth Specialties, 1224 Greenfield, El Cajon, CA 92021.

CHAPTER TWO

SETTING THE DIRECTION FOR YOUR MINISTRY

By DARRELL PEARSON

As I was beginning to write this chapter, I received a call from a youth leader at another church who asked if my church had any youth policies. I wasn't sure what she meant, but as we talked, I realized that she wanted my "whys and why nots" for youth ministry, not the "regulations and rules." Her church had no idea what it was trying to accomplish with its junior high group. My encouragement to her was to start with a clearly defined philosophy of ministry.

PHILOSOPHY OF JUNIOR HIGH MINISTRY

You and your church might already have one in place, but I am often surprised at how rarely I find youth workers who have thought through the philosophy of what they are attempting to do. Are you trying to develop disciples through one-on-one ministry? Reach out to new kids through outreach programs? Build a ministry that is low-key and primarily relational? Develop student leadership? Involve students in the lives of the adult church members? Every church and every situation is different, so there is no correct or incorrect philosophy, but—whatever it is—it must be spelled out clearly, or you will have no concept of what you are setting goals for.

A number of years ago I spent a few days interviewing a number of youth directors from churches that are well known for having strong youth programs. Every person I talked with was able to pull a philosophy of ministry out of a file and hand me a copy. One church built its outreach ministry on a model where a high-profile program brought kids to church; one was structured around student-led small group Bible studies; and the others had vastly different ideas as well. All of them, however, knew why they were doing what they were doing. Too often churches build their junior high ministries around simply occupying kids' time, rather than trying to accomplish something significant. What do you *really* want to see happen?

Try and locate a philosophy of ministry that represents what your church as a whole is trying to do. If you can't find a specific one for the entire church, try the Christian Education program. You are likely to discover a statement somewhere that describes what your church is attempting to do and how it can be accomplished. When you find it, summarize it below.

_____
_____
_____
_____
_____

If you have a hard time locating a statement like this, answer the following questions from your own observations:

1. What would you say is the main purpose of your church (worship, outreach, education, and so on)?
2. In which areas is your church doing well (strong music ministry, great youth program, welcoming visitors . . .)?

Write your own philosophy of your church's overall ministry based on your observations about how ministry is happening.

To identify your church's junior high philosophy of ministry (not youth ministry in general and not senior high), answer the following questions:

1. In which specific areas does it *appear*

that your church wants to put an emphasis in junior high (involvement in worship services, keeping the kids out of the adults' hair, service trips, youth choir, and so forth)?
2. In which specific areas is your junior high ministry doing well?

Write your own philosophy of your overall junior high ministry based on your observations.

Now, compare your church's overall philosophy with your junior high philosophy. Are the two in harmony? How might they correlate better? If your church's philosophy rests heavily on outreach, is the junior high ministry also oriented this way, or is the program directed only to in-house students? If you need to write out a new junior high philosophy that accurately reflects where your ministry needs to be, take the time to do it before you move any further. If you are not sure how to do it, note the example that follows. Your philosophy doesn't have to be similar or focus on the same areas, it just needs to be centered on your situation and what your church needs to be doing in junior high ministry.

A PHILOSOPHY OF JUNIOR HIGH MINISTRY

The junior high ministry, under the guidelines of Ephesians 4:11–13, seeks to enable two groups of individuals for ministry: 1) Junior high students, that they may gain an understanding of themselves as the body of Christ, able to be learners, leaders, teachers, and stewards in the context of the world in which they live, and 2) Volunteer adults, that they may gain an understanding of the validity and necessity of youth ministry, experience the joy of serving Christ through their involvement with youths, and learn to effectively minister to young people. The junior high ministry strives to minister to the whole person, is based on relationships, is designed to minister to

needs, and is creatively programmed to meet these needs.

This philosophy results in a practical program of ministry.

The junior high ministry, under the guidelines of Ephesians 4:11-13,

It was he who gave some to be apostles, some to be prophets, some to be evangelists, and some to be pastors and teachers, to prepare God's people for works of service, so that the body of Christ may be built up until we all reach unity in the faith and in the knowledge of the Son of God and become mature, attaining to the whole measure of the fullness of Christ.

seeks to enable two groups of individuals for ministry: 1) Junior high students, that they may gain an understanding of themselves as the body of Christ,

Students assume responsibilities in the life of the church: worship, tithing, membership, service projects, and fellowship.

able to be learners,

Students attend Sunday school classes, Wednesday electives, and Bible study.

leaders,

Quarterly planning groups design their own programs, and students do up-front leading (announcements, skits, prayer).

teachers,

Students participate in drama and choir performances, assist teachers in the children's department, and assist adult leaders in electives.

and stewards,

Students give to the missions of their choosing and learn to use their gifts in ministry through music and drama.

in the context of the world in which they live.

Curriculum is designed and adapted to meet the needs of students growing up in the nineties and to prepare them for roles as Christian leaders in adulthood.

2) Volunteer adults, that they may gain an understanding of the validity and necessity of youth ministry,

Involvement gives adults relationships with kids, allowing them to see growth and results in youths and to see the impact of their own modeling and leading.

experience the joy of serving Christ through their involvement with youths,

Service in the name of Christ provides volunteers meaning and application for their faith.

and learn to effectively minister to young people.

Adults attend quarterly teacher training sessions. Their opportunities for fellowship include teacher dinners and retreats. Adequate age-level curriculum is found and evaluation is done. Responsibility for ministry is ultimately in the hands of the volunteer.

The junior high ministry strives to minister to the whole person,

Along with spiritual development, opportunities are offered for physical, mental, and social development.

is based on relationships,

Relational ministry is at the root of the program. Students have relationships with adults through the small-group classes and electives and they build relationships with each other through diverse activities.

is designed to minister to needs,

Ministry is based on needs, not just of junior highers in general, but on the specific needs of students in our church. Kids have need of relationships, understanding the church in relation to themselves, developmental needs, physical needs, and emotional needs unique to early adolescence.

and is creatively programmed to meet these needs.

Theme nights, retreats, creative Bible teaching, media, program material designed by staff and volunteers, all demonstrate creative programming aimed at reaching junior high students in the 1990s.

SET YOUR GOALS

Now you are ready to move ahead with specific directions through goal setting. I like to start with the "big dreams" for the year ahead—those ministries that will give kids a great sense of accomplishment and learning. What unbelievable things could you do that would have a lasting impact on your students? Write a couple of ideas down here.

My big dream is . . .

Another dream would be . . .

Last year as I contemplated my big dreams, I was motivated by the idea of accomplishing two major new programs. First, I wanted my kids in drama to be able to present a production that would influence the whole church. We decided to do *Fiddler on the Roof*, which is seemingly impossible to do with junior highers (too many adult male roles), but we did it with great success. A ninth grade missions trip to Mexico also grew out of a big dream idea and became reality. Although I am committed to week-by-week ministry, the big dream ideas are the ones that get remembered. Are you frustrated with your group? Does Sunday morning get to be a major drag and seem totally uncreative? Challenge your kids with a big dream. If you work with a small youth group, don't be afraid to dream big, too. You could plan a trip that every student could be a part of or a youth night for your church that really shows the adult population what kids are capable of doing. Dream big!

Once your big dreams are thought through, get specific with short- and long-range goals. *Fiddler on the Roof* required the long-range planning of a rehearsal schedule that didn't leave the kids worn out at the last minute and that also fit the church's facilities calendar. It took several of us two solid days of analyzing the script to create a rehearsal schedule that used kids' time appropriately. When planning programs like midweek meetings, camps, and activities, specific long-range goals make them happen.

Short-range goals are necessary, too: They help you accomplish things in the short term of less than one month. By clearly defining both, you are on your way to creating some important experiences for your group.

Take a moment now, and sketch out several long-range goals that might help your big dreams to become realities.

Long-range goal #1 (Be specific!)

_____

Long-range goal #2

_____

Now write in a couple of short-range goals that might help the long-range plan become reality.

Short-range goal #1

_____

Short-range goal #2

_____

The following example shows how this might all work together:

> The Big Dream: You want your junior highers to stretch their limits physically and spiritually through an activity that they have never done before—a 200-mile bike trip.
> Long-range goals:
> Schedule a week in July.
> Make sure the church van is available!
> Put several preparatory meetings on the calendar for April and May.
> Short-range goals:
> Pick ten key kids in the group and get their responses to the idea.
> Take a one-day bike trip to determine the kids' limits (and your own!).

Being specific with your goals will help make your big dreams come true. If you can spell out the dream, your goals will naturally fall into place. They have to or you'll never accomplish that great idea.

THE PLANNING PROCESS

Day-to-day ministry doesn't always fall under the big dream concept. We all have to continue to come up with creative ideas for Friday, Wednesday, Sunday, or any time that's right around the corner. A planning process is invaluable to make the everyday ideas work.

One friend of mine uses the following planning sheet (found on p. 33) to make sure he gets what needs to be done, done.

For shorter planning (things happening within a few days), I like to use the following process sheet (found on p. 34). It helps a nondetail-oriented person like me remember the little things I need to know.

Here's a small warning about group planning. Most junior high leaders today are involving their students more in the planning process so that there is ownership of the program by the kids. The problem is that kids have a limited view of their own needs and tend to plan programs that are somewhat shortsighted. It is easy to end up with eight summer trips to the amusement park when you know that what they need is more Bible study. Personally, I like to involve my kids in brainstorming ideas for a specific program or event rather than for the overall picture. Planning for the big picture is my job; motivating and placing kids in program leadership then follows. Be careful when allowing kids to be a part of the planning process—they are best off enjoying being a part of something you have carefully created.

MAINTAINING BALANCE

There are a number of areas that need to stay in balance as you begin creating your programs. All of us have natural biases that tend to make us lean too far in one direction or the other.

FUN VERSUS SERIOUS. No matter how many parents tell you their kids need more straight Bible teaching, remember that junior highers need to have fun at just about everything. Don't feel guilty planning forty-five minutes of fun and fifteen minutes of serious during an hour-long program. Of course, it's easy sometimes to forget that serious angle

ITEM	DATE NEEDED	COMPLETED (X)
Theme selection		
Flyer		
Counselor selection		
Parent letter		
Promotional copy		
Speaker		
Campers' booklets		
Bible studies		
Counselors' manuals		
Music		
Leaders' meetings		
Camp schedule		
Seminars		
Afternoon activities		
Evening activities		
Camp sign-up		
Cabin lists		
Final count to camp facility		
Insurance forms		
Confirmation cards and maps		
Video		

EVENT _____

PAGE _____ OF _____

Time (Date)	Activity	Person Responsible	Location	Materials	Comments

and just have a great time. Don't be guilty of going overboard in either direction—keep it balanced!

HIGH ENERGY VERSUS LOW ENERGY. Most people think of junior highers as being always off the wall and completely crazy. Although this can be true—and you need to create programming that lets them run, climb, and destroy—you also need the balance of times when they don't go nuts. Their young and growing bodies need to relax and sit occasionally.

Years ago, my philosophy on the first night of a retreat was to run the kids through a variety of games to burn up their energy and wear them down so they'd sleep. Many times the games either hyped them up more so they couldn't slow down later, or we had a rash of injuries as the kids got tired. Now, I rarely have kids run much on the first night. Many weekends they are already so tired from the week at school that they need to slow the pace down a little. Of course, regardless of whether we play games or not, they still talk half the night away!

LARGE GROUP VERSUS SMALL GROUP. Junior highers need to experience the intimacy (or at least the attempt toward intimacy) of a small group, but they also need the excitement of a large group setting once in a while. If your group is small (potential attendance of under twenty-five), you have the built-in ability for each kid to be "known." It might seem boring to you sometimes, but at least you have a manageable setting that allows you to get a handle on who every person is. But this is not enough for a balanced ministry. You also need some large group experiences so your kids know what it's like to be a part of the larger

Christian body. Have an activity with several other churches now and then—go to a Christian concert, participate in a regional interdenominational gathering, or go to a summer camp that involves lots of other kids. Junior highers need to feel like there is something happening.

If you have a large group, the opposite is true. Although it's fun and exciting to have a big group at your events, remember that every student you have has a desperate longing for someone to know who she or he is. Make sure you break your group down into smaller cells led by other adults. Sunday classes by age or topic, impromptu discussion groups, and share nights for kids wanting to talk about deeper issues all help find the balance of large group versus small group.

SCHEDULED VERSUS SPONTANEOUS. The most creative junior high program in the universe just might not work—if it happens to be held on the wrong night in the junior high world. Be ready and willing to change from the scheduled activity to the spontaneous.

One of my greatest bizarre and crazy nights was planned for a certain Wednesday that happened to fall the day after the spaceship *Challenger* blew up. I was determined to pull off an evening that I had invested a lot of time preparing. In fact, I figured the kids were overwhelmed with the media coverage of the crash and ready for a break—wrong! They were intense that night: thoughtful, introspective, wanting to spend time praying and thinking about life (praying! thinking!). There was no recourse but to change the night around and go with the flow.

This doesn't mean that you can approach a program night thinking you will "just be spontaneous" because the kids need it (great excuse for not planning well!). It does mean that you may have to put aside your most creative effort to change according to the mood of the students. I am still waiting for one of the many knowledgeable computer buffs I know to write me a program that accurately predicts my students' moods each week. Until that happens, though, I'll just be ready to be spontaneous.

The element of surprise can be unbelievable with junior highers. Sometimes the best scheduled idea is one that the kids *think* is spontaneous. Years ago my predecessor had the police stop the church bus on the way to a retreat and frisk the leaders. It was carefully planned, but the kids were totally surprised! It was an unforgettable way to introduce the topic for the weekend.

BASICS VERSUS IN-DEPTH. Another area to keep in mind as you plan creatively is to make sure that you are teaching the simple basics of the Christian faith, yet challenging the students skilled in the basics to grow even deeper. It is easy to keep focusing on the issues of friendship; relating to God; or coping with school, parents, sex, and so on. But how about something different once in a while? Why not take a meeting to explore male/female biblical roles, abortion, Bible memory, cults, or women in the ministry—something a little meatier for the kids who need more challenge.

I remember a summer camp several years ago when our evening topic was spiritual gifts. When Susie took her ninth grade girls back to the cabin, they launched into the issue of the blasphemy of the Holy Spirit. Susie was shocked at the abrupt change, overwhelmed by their sudden interest, and pleased that they

were concerned about their futures with God. These girls did some heavy thinking and needed some direction, not just at camp, but on our return home as well.

If you are the "heady" type, make sure you have time for talking about how to *know* Jesus personally. If you are the type that focuses on the basics, look at a scary and unsure topic once in a while.

INTELLECTUAL VERSUS EMOTIONAL. Find that balance between intellectual and emotional. Lead your kids to understand their God and to feel something about that God and themselves. There are times when junior highers, who so often have such intense emotions, need to feel something about their faith, even though we like to tell them (and we know it's true) that they can't depend on feelings. If it's all knowledge, they won't have the proper balance of also feeling their faith.

In my personal study time and even in my worship experiences, I tend to focus on the intellectual side of the faith because I know it is more dependable than feelings. But recently at a youth pastor's seminar, the time of worship was a refreshing experience for me. I *felt* like I was worshipping God and he was speaking to me. Is that so bad? Of course not. Junior highers need to feel even more than I that God is out there and that he cares for them.

If you have worked through this chapter and jotted a few ideas down, the direction you plan to move in should start to take form. Once you have a reason to do what you plan to do (philosophy) and the needs of your kids and how you'll meet them are figured out (goals), then you are ready to start programming the details (the planning process) with the proper perspective (balance) in mind.

CHAPTER THREE

DEVELOPING YOUR CREATIVE POWERS

By DARRELL PEARSON

Whenever I mention the concept of developing creativity, more often than not the response is, "Yeah, right; you don't know me. I'm just not a creative person." Well, I don't believe it for a moment. *Everyone* has some creative powers—people just don't always recognize them. Try this on: The Creator of the entire world, the One who has brilliantly and perfectly made everything that exists, the God who added so many special touches to his works, is the same God who made each of us in his image. If he's creative, so are we! We just have to figure out how to tap those creative areas. You might be the one to create the next classic youth idea that other junior high workers have dreamed about. It starts with a few simple guidelines.

YOU: THE KING OR QUEEN OF CREATIVITY

Take a moment to think through your past creative efforts. Which ones are you proud of? It might be something at your job, something you created with your hands, or that unbelievable art project you did in the second grade that your mother saved. List them here:

Creative success #1

_____

Creative success #2

_____

Creative success #3

_____

Now, give yourself some credit; certainly you have done something in the past that qualifies as creative genius. The problem many have at this point is jumping the gap to junior high ministry. I believe that if you can recognize the creative impulses you've had in other areas in your life, you can create new and exciting program ideas for junior high students.

My friend Randy spends most of his working hours constructing buildings. He doesn't consider himself particularly creative, especially when it comes to teaching his junior high Sunday school class each week at his little church in the mountains. But Randy's craftsmanship with wood is superb—he can make beautiful things from a very simple piece of aspen. Recently he told me, with a gleam in his eye, how he built a wall from scratch during forty-five minutes of class time to illustrate laying our lives on a good foundation and structure. He *is* creative; he just had to learn how to transfer that to junior high students.

IT TAKES TIME TO CREATE

Developing creativity takes an investment of time to allow the juices to flow. Ten minutes before your junior highers arrive for the evening program is probably not the time that it's going to happen (although, there are moments . . .). To effectively develop creativity, you have to designate periods of time when you actively seek creative solutions and ideas. A planning-and-retreat day away from the usual schedule often helps; occasional trips to unusual places to generate some enthusiasm work, too. If you want to be creative, make the time!

OBSERVING

Yogi Berra, the great malapropism creator, is famous for the statement, "You can observe a lot by just watching!" It's an unusual way to say it, but it's true. If you take the time to watch the world around you, you can observe enough to fill your mind with unlimited creative ideas. As you live each day, observe what happens around you and consider its impact on junior high programming. Watch the commercials, the fads, the people; listen to the words people say—anything that will give you an edge on creating something fantastic for junior high kids.

For example, I like to wander periodically through my local supermarket and see what interesting things come to mind (you know how well junior highers and food go together!). This might seem like a waste of time at first, but it is worth the effort. Steve is great at this—he calls it "creative loafing." As you enter the store, head for the produce section. Have you noticed what a great variety of foods are available here—many of which are relatively new to American tastes? What can you do with kiwi fruit? Star fruit? Standard items like tomatoes, watermelons, or pineapples? Eating contests come to mind, as do relays where you carry the fruit to the next person. Perhaps you could cut up a vegetable to see what's inside (an illustration of our inner selves). The possibilities are endless.

Now move to the next aisle. Everything's generic! Hmmm . . . a great way to introduce the topic of studying gray areas. Are there any issues that always have black and white answers? How about dressing up for Generic Night—everyone must be in nonlabeled clothes, absent of color. Use generic brands to talk about our need to have status names on our clothes, or discuss how real servants don't need their names attached to good deeds.

Let's try the meat department. A chicken (or a rubber facsimile) has interesting possibilities for games. Have you ever tried chicken volleyball? It works for a hilarious, but short, five minutes. Tap into the biblical concept of eating meat instead of living on milk. Showing a beef heart on Sunday will add an interesting touch to your lesson.

Every aisle has possibilities, but you have to make time to walk those aisles and take notes. Food is a dramatic way to emphasize issues of world hunger and our resources. Why not take your kids to the supermarket, give each group five bucks, and see who can feed the most people a nutritious meal? The grocery store is just one place you can travel for ideas, and the ideas are endless.

Take the room you are sitting in now (if you are indeed reading this in a room—I suppose you could be in a supermarket). Look around you. What ideas can you generate from observing the room? See the lamp across the room with the burned-out bulb? What did Jesus say about lamps on a stand? Or take the outlet—it makes a dramatic illustration of tapping into the power source (we don't see electricity, but watch it work when I plug in this blender with the top off . . .). Of course, there's the television and stereo; have you talked with your students about making wise entertainment choices?

Jot down the names of objects from a variety of rooms on the worksheet below. Then, next to each item write a possible study topic or game that it brings to mind.

If the items you noted

ROOM: LIVING ROOM
Interesting objects:

Ideas . . .

ROOM: SOMEBODY'S OFFICE
Interesting objects:

Ideas . . .

ROOM: KITCHEN
Interesting objects:

Ideas . . .

PLACE: (Pick something unusual: a 7-Eleven store, a bowling alley, anything)
Interesting objects:

Ideas . . .

Creativity Tip: Think through the alphabet one letter at a time and see what each letter stimulates you to create in a given program area. For example, if the category was discussion ideas, "A" might stand for *attitudes, achievement,* or *answers,* all of which might make interesting discussion topics.

don't bring much to mind, try them on a friend or a fellow junior high worker. They might be able to take your concept and develop the practical end of things that you can't seem to create.

Look around you! The creative ideas are there, if you spend some effort looking. Remember, you can observe a lot by just watching.

THE IDEA FILE

Have you ever driven down the road, noticed a billboard that gave you an idea, and then later couldn't remember the brilliant idea no matter how hard you tried? Ideas need to be recorded. Keep paper and a pencil handy, and record every thought so it doesn't disappear. (I keep tiny sheets in my wallet, but I'm still searching for the small flexible pencil that doesn't break when I sit down!) You might want to carry a dictaphone when you don't have a pen and paper handy. Then, drop your notes into a special file reserved for creative thoughts. Tear ideas out of the newspaper or a magazine that you might be able to use later. I just saved the clipping from a mail-order house that specializes in bizarre objects (I think they are bizarre, but maybe you buy nose clippers all the time), and I plan to order some of these items. Better yet, I think I'll let the kids decide which items to order once a month, then we can all get excited when the package arrives with our group's personalized dog jacket. The point is, if it's not recorded and dropped in the file, it's not likely to happen.

TAKING RISKS

To be creative, you have to be willing to risk some failure. Sometimes your most amazing idea turns out to be a total bomb. That's okay! The next one might be a winner. If you don't try it, you'll never learn how to judge a creative idea.

I had an intern ten years ago who still teases me about an idea that didn't quite work. (I still think it was a good idea, but the wrong kids must have been in the room.) I was speaking to my group on how to use available tools to understand the Bible (a Bible dictionary, an atlas, and so on). To make my point, I stuffed numerous tools in strange places in the suit I was wearing. A tiny jeweler's saw, a large crosscut, and a small electric drill were among the items stored in my pockets, up my back, and up my pant leg. As I pulled each tool out, the kids got quieter and quieter and stared at me rather strangely. They thought they had a youth minister, and it turned out they had a modified Mr. Goodwrench. Instead of making a point, I just came across as a complete geek. Okay, so it didn't work, and Alan was right—but at least I tried. It was soon forgotten when several weeks later I hung precariously from the balcony as Alan tore his suit off to reveal a Superman costume. (You can guess the rest.) Be willing to give your creative efforts a try!

Sometimes risking means letting others try their ideas, even when you think they won't work. Give your volunteers the freedom to give it a shot—you don't know when it will pay off, but the risk is something you must often take.

When John came to me with his ideas for a serious ninth grade approach to Sunday school (he wanted to adapt an adult Bible study program for junior high), I was somewhat skeptical, especially when I prejudged him as being too quiet and not particularly creative. But when I saw his product, which was well organized and challenging to students, I became a believer. Kids loved his class because he made them think. I later learned that he was an expert simulation games creator in his school classroom (more on simulations in Chapter Nine), and he often created learning games that stretched over several weeks. It seemed risky, but it was worth the try.

THINKING THEMATICALLY

Junior high students love, and respond to, themes. Think through today's fads and consider what you can do with these ideas. TV shows, movies, and products that are marketed to teens all present ministry opportunities. As I think back on my years in junior high ministry, I can visualize some memorable theme nights we did that corresponded to the times.

Rubik's Cube Night (that was a long time ago!)
Setting the world record for the largest "Uno" game (we were the only group who tried)
"Battle of the Network Superstars"
Break Dancing
"American Gladiators"

Something new is always happening. Last year my adult leaders were lamenting that it had been a long time since we visited Disneyland, so we re-created our own version of the great theme park. A lot of the "rides" were strange and silly, but "Star Tours" was hot! We had fun putting the event on, though it took a lot of hard work.

RESOURCES FOR CREATIVITY

Although there are many places to find great ideas, the following are a few good resources to tap:

PUBLISHED RESOURCES. Go to the Christian bookstore and look in the youth section. Buy anything you can afford that looks like it's interesting. There are many printed resources that are helpful: Group's *Junior High Ministry* magazine has many good ideas, and Youth Specialties' classic *Ideas* books are full of

great suggestions. Write *Chases Calendar of Events*[1] for a copy of their latest book that lists national holidays for every day of the year. Order a copy of Marlene LeFever's book, *Creative Teaching Methods*.[2] Seek—and you will find good resources.

ADAPTING THOSE RESOURCES. Now, reality sets in. Most good materials don't quite fit the needs of your group. Feel free to adapt them to make them work. Most good ideas need a small nudge to be great.

SWIPING FROM YOUR FRIENDS. If you don't know others in junior high ministry, go and meet them! One of the best resources is junior high workers at other churches. Head to your state's Sunday school convention or a specific resource seminar designed for youth leaders. When you meet other people, you will pick up many new ideas just from casual interchange. No one in your group will ever know that you borrowed that great discussion tool from someone else. They will only remember that it was a great idea.

STORYBOARDING

This is quite possibly the best format for discovering creative ideas by yourself and with a group. The concept comes from Mike Vance, who in his series *Creative Thinking*,[3] shows a simple format for developing creativity. Basically, it involves a bulletin board, push pins, and two-by-three-inch cards (a plain wall and sticky notes can be substituted). I became sold on the idea when an architect told me how his company created the facility in which my church is housed by using this technique. They storyboarded all the concepts and needs on their walls and then designed a building to meet the needs. Here's how it works.

As you brainstorm with a group of people, one person writes on a small card the concepts submitted (one concept per card). The leader pins the card to the wall. As more ideas are created, the pins are moved around appropriately. Let's say we are creating a weekend retreat on the theme "Spiritual Warfare." The leader asks for any random ideas on the subject (no idea should be rejected yet), then the cards are pinned on the board. After several minutes, the board might look like this.

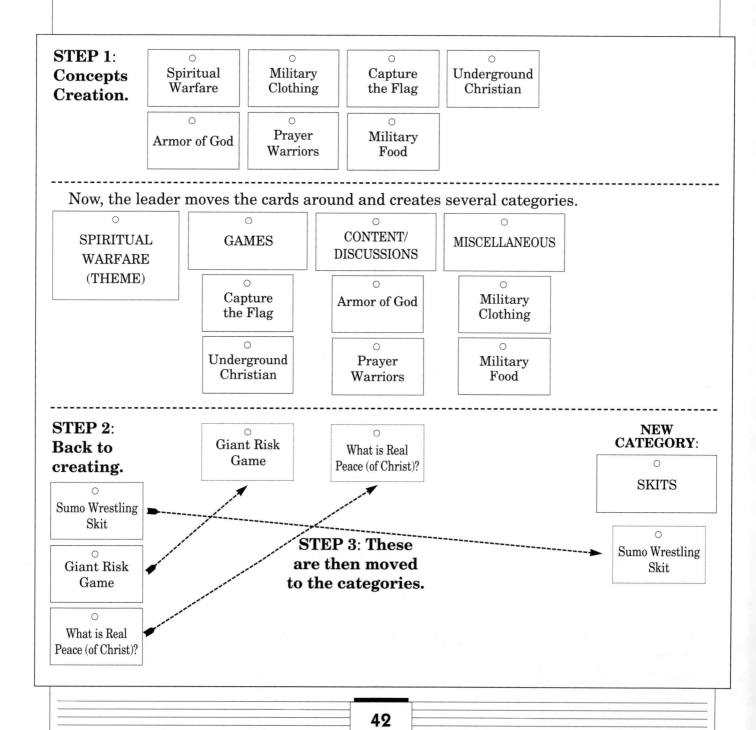

STEP 1: Concepts Creation.

Spiritual Warfare | Military Clothing | Capture the Flag | Underground Christian

Armor of God | Prayer Warriors | Military Food

Now, the leader moves the cards around and creates several categories.

SPIRITUAL WARFARE (THEME) | GAMES | CONTENT/ DISCUSSIONS | MISCELLANEOUS

Capture the Flag | Armor of God | Military Clothing

Underground Christian | Prayer Warriors | Military Food

STEP 2: Back to creating.

Giant Risk Game

What is Real Peace (of Christ)?

NEW CATEGORY:

SKITS

Sumo Wrestling Skit

Giant Risk Game

What is Real Peace (of Christ)?

STEP 3: These are then moved to the categories.

Sumo Wrestling Skit

The process moves on, and the ideas are endless. After creating a wealth of concepts, evaluate what is useable, practical, and realistic. You will find it's now hard to eliminate ideas, when before it was hard to find them.

I always keep two storyboards in my office. One is reserved for planning specific events, such as the Wednesday night program, a retreat, or the casting of a play. The other board is ongoing: When an idea comes to mind, I write it on a card and pin it on the board. It is a great help to my sometimes slow creative process!

The system from Mike Vance is available from Nightingale/Conant Corporation, 3730 W. Devon Avenue, Chicago, IL 60659. Vance also teaches frequent seminars on the fine details of the process.

Creativity—sometimes it seems so elusive, and yet the ideas are there if we put out the effort and give it a try. We all have creative abilities; we just need to learn how to direct them into the bizarre world of junior high ministry.

ENDNOTES

1. *Chases Calendar of Events*, Apple Tree Press, P.O. Box 1012, Flint, MI 48501.
2. Marlene LeFever, *Creative Teaching Methods: Be An Effective Christian Teacher* (Elgin, Ill.: David C. Cook, 1985).
3. Mike Vance, *Creative Thinking* (Chicago: Nightingale/Conant, 1982).

CHAPTER FOUR

CREATIVE TEACHING, TITLES, AND TOPICS

By STEVE DICKIE

My favorite part of our Sunday morning church service is the children's sermon. That is when the pastor invites the children forward for a brief mini-message. From what I have heard from many other adults, it's their favorite time, too. Why? Besides the fun of watching kids, I'm convinced that people like hearing Christian truth taught creatively. It is fresh, usually to the point, and often framed with creative stories and props. It becomes a wonderful moment (often in the midst of boring tradition) when creativity is allowed to flourish.

Frankly, I've always wondered why it takes such a bold move to toss touches of creativity into our church services. There's nothing wrong with tradition—it provides security and consistency in its structure—I just wish we'd be more open to the creative possibilities that are available to us. Jesus was a great example of creative teaching. He was a master at using analogy, stories, location, and object illustration in his communication. This should allow us to "loosen up" and to let ourselves test the creative waters. Jesus did it.

The good news is that youth workers are usually given a fair amount of freedom to use creativity in their teaching. I guess others expect it from us. Is it our superior theological understanding, or are we just bizarre, outrageous, and a little bit out of control? Actually, the nature of who we are teaching demands it. If we want to be effective in junior high ministry, we must use every means available to us. Not too sure where to start? No problem. With a little smart organization you can do a great job, keep the kids interested, and have fun to boot. Here are a few ideas on choosing the right direction.

CHOOSING TO UNDERSTAND A FEW BASIC PRINCIPLES

Teaching is important. We want to do well because we want kids to grow in their relationships with Jesus. I heard a youth worker once describe her task as "loving kids, loving God, and loving to help kids love God." To accomplish this, it's wise to understand how kids best learn from our teaching.

Bill McNabb and Steven Mabry, in their wonderful book *Teaching the Bible Creatively: How to Awaken Your Kids to Scripture,*[1] discuss how students best learn. Their fourteen principles give us a good guide on how to best direct our teaching efforts. Good stuff!

1. Kids are motivated to learn by learning.
2. Kids learn better when they experience.
3. Kids learn better in a comfortable environment.
4. Kids learn better when they discuss what they are learning.
5. Kids believe what they do more than they do what they believe.
6. Kids are motivated to learn when the answer is not obvious.
7. Kids learn better when the focus is on the concrete.
8. Kids learn better when they help to choose what they study.
9. Kids learn better when they can translate terms into their own language.
10. Kids learn better when they are challenged to be creative.
11. Kids learn better in varied settings.
12. Kids learn better under the guidance of a Christian mentor.
13. Kids learn better from teachers who care about them.
14. Kids learn more when their lessons affect their lives.

CHOOSING YOUR COMMUNICATION STYLE

Obviously, there are a variety of communication styles. Choosing the appropriate method usually depends on the needs of your group. Here are some possibilities with a few of their pluses and minuses.

LECTURE. A message, talk, or sermon delivered to an audience. *Plus:* Lecturing is an easy way to address a large audience. *Minuses:* It doesn't allow much interaction, it can be boring if the leader has poor speaking abilities, and students' attention can drift easily.

DIRECTED DISCUSSION. An interaction between the leader and the group members in which the leader directs the "flow" toward a designed end. *Plus:* It keeps the group involved through participation and allows the group to express opinions. *Minuses:* It is dependent upon a leader's discussion-leading abilities, many groups are more used to listening than discussing, and it is difficult with very large groups.

FREE DISCUSSION. An interaction in which the leader allows the discussion to head in any direction. Wherever it ends up is okay. *Pluses:* It can be fun, and it allows kids to share things that they haven't had the opportunity to express. *Minuses:* Sometimes the group is slow to open up, and it is easy to lose control if the leader isn't skilled.

BODY LIFE. Similar to free discussion in that it lets what happens happen. The group (body) ministers to each other through the sharing of needs, group prayer, singing, and worship. *Plus:* The

Holy Spirit is allowed to run the meeting. *Minus:* It often takes time for a group to learn to "flow."

SMALL GROUP. The group is broken into small units. *Pluses:* It allows for more personal interaction and for needs to be expressed and heard. *Minus:* Some kids are shy about expressing their thoughts.

ROLE-PLAY. Members of the group act out real-life situations by putting themselves in roles. *Pluses:* High participation, it is fun and interesting to watch, and kids must think through other points of view. *Minuses:* It requires a good role-play situation, and some kids need prodding to participate.

CASE STUDY. A real-life situation is shared or read. Usually the ending is left open. The kids discuss, offer opinions, or try to figure out the best end result. *Pluses:* High involvement, it allows for a variety of opinions, and the group often identifies with the situations. *Minus:* You need good, real-life case studies.

LEARNING GAME. A game that teaches a principle, usually followed by the group discussing what it has learned. *Pluses:* It is fun and a great discussion starter. *Minus:* It takes a lot of work to find or to dream up a good game that deals with your topic.

OBJECT LESSONS. Physical objects are used to illustrate and communicate a point. *Pluses:* These are fun and usually easy to come up with, they attract and hold attention, and they cause the group to remember your point. *Minus:* They can detract from your point if overemphasized.

DRAMA. Acting can be a wonderful teaching and learning experience for both the actors and the audience. A small drama is a natural setup for a discussion or a talk (see Chapter Twelve for some specific ideas). *Pluses:* Drama is very visual and useful when it is used to complement other teaching styles. *Minus:* It requires preparation and practice.

ART. Drawings and pictures are used to illustrate a concept or a message. *Pluses:* Art taps into the creativity of kids or leaders who have art talent, it is very visual, it sets a mood, and it can linger over time—it reminds the kids of truth wherever they see it. *Minus:* The participants must enjoy expressing themselves through art and have an element of artistic talent.

WRITING. Kids learn by writing down their thoughts in such ways as journaling, letters to God, poetry, prose, or self-expression. *Pluses:* Kids can express themselves at their own level of reflection, they can keep their work, and it opens up a lot of opportunities for creative expression. *Minuses:* Some junior highers don't have good writing or expressive skills, and many kids don't have the patience or the discipline to stick with it.

READING. Read Scripture, magazines, books, and other printed material. *Pluses:* Each kid can work at his or her own pace, level, and time schedule; Scripture reading is core to spiritual growth; and an abundance of quality Christian reading is aimed at youth audiences. *Minuses:* Reading requires discipline, some leaders don't know where to access good youth-oriented material, and some kids have the misconception that the Bible is boring.

VISUAL MEDIA. This includes a variety of media, such as film, video, slides, filmstrip, and the like. *Pluses:* It is very visual; kids often view it as a treat; you can buy, rent, or create your own; and there's a multitude of things you can do with it. *Minuses:* Equipment costs money, and some leaders don't know how to access quality resources.

MUSIC. Listen to or express all kinds of music. *Pluses:* Music can teach Christian truth, it is an excellent way to memorize Scripture, and there is an amazing amount of excellent Christian resources. *Minuses:* Some leaders don't know how to access the resources, some kids feel too awkward or embarrassed to sing, you need a person with some musical talent to lead in the expression of music, and some kids are slow to understand that recorded Christian music is good *and* cool.

WORKSHEETS. Preprinted questions allow kids to write in responses. They can also research Scripture passages and record their answers and thoughts. *Pluses:* The leader can direct the responses toward a specific target, each kid can work at her or his own pace, it allows for expression of personal opinion, and it is private. *Minuses:* It's a little too much like school, the leader has to be wise in asking questions that flow together, and it can become "ammo" when used in a classroom setting (better to use as take-home follow-up).

MEMORY. Take Scripture and put it to memory. It can be done as a group or individually at home. *Pluses:* There are many creative ways to memorize—music, pictures, and so on; it puts Scripture in the kids' minds and hearts; and it can be fun when tapped into creative options. *Minus:* The leader has to express positive enthusiasm so it doesn't appear too much like school.

QUIZZING. Quiz students on things they previously learned. *Pluses:* It can be fun if done creatively (game show for-mat), and it reinforces learning. *Minuses:* Kids could become fearful if they think they'll be embarrassed, and it can appear too much like school.

ON-SITE LEARNING. Use your location to teach. *Pluses:* It's fun and sometimes adventurous; it's something different and out-of-the-ordinary; there are a multitude of resources (including nature itself); all the senses are used; and it allows kids to do, not just to hear. *Minuses:* It requires advance planning, transportation, chaperons, and time.

MENTORING (DISCIPLESHIP). Teach kids by lifestyle example (see Chapter Ten). *Pluses:* This can happen simply in the way we live as well as by specific design, it is modeled by the life of Christ, many excellent resources are available, kids *want* to spend time with us, and this teaching tool lasts a lifetime. *Minuses:* It requires our time and consistency.

BIBLE STUDY. The truth of God's Word can be taught in a variety of ways. These include deductive study, inductive study, word study, and theme study. *Pluses:* A variety of methods can be used for teaching, countless resources are available at all levels, and this is the core of the Christian faith. *Minuses:* Some leaders unfortunately don't know the Bible, and some leaders aren't confident in teaching the Bible.

COMBINATION. Use a combination of many of these styles. *Pluses:* It would probably be most effective, it offers lots of variety, it allows for freedom of adjustment when needs change, it gives the leader countless alternatives and resources, and kids are kept interested while the leader avoids a rut. *Minuses:* The leader must research all options available, the leader needs to avoid being a "one style" person, and the leader may not have strengths in some areas.

CHOOSING TEACHING TITLES

One of my favorite things about teaching is coming up with creative titles for my topics. Besides the fun of dreaming up titles, it is also pretty smart (if I do say so myself). A good title accomplishes a variety of things: It can spark kids' interest in the topic, it can "charge up" a subject or a passage that they might otherwise show little enthusiasm for, and it can help them remember the topic and content later. Here are ten favorites that I've come up with over the years (okay, they're corny, but they're still my favorites).

ANGER. "Don't Be a Fool and Try to be Cool, By Picking a Fight with Someone Named Abdul."

TEMPTATION. "What Do You Do, When You Want to Do, the Things You Know, You Shouldn't Do?" (can double as a rap)

SELF-ESTEEM. "The Totallyradicalwonderfulme!" (my favorite)

FAILURE AND DEFEAT. "If Failure Helps Me Grow, Then Why Do I Feel So Rotten?"

ADVICE ON DATING FOR BOYS. "Wise Words for Wiseguys."

SHYNESS. "Public Speaking Gives Me Acne."

JEALOUSY. "Drowning in the Jealous Sea." (get it?)

STRESS. "Aaaaaaarrrrrrrgggggggghhhhhhhhh!"

DANIEL 3. "The Adventures of Biff, Bud, and Bob."

GENESIS 38. "This Passage Sticks Out Like a Cow with a Fifth Leg." (You have to read this passage to understand it.)

Coming up with creative titles really isn't all that difficult. I actually think it's fun. The following are a few helpful ways I get my "creative title brainstorming juices" flowing:

1. I ask for ideas. The secretaries in my office love helping me come up with titles. They're pretty good at it, too.

2. I go to bookstores (especially Christian bookstores) and look at book titles and chapter headings. I can glean quite a few ideas that become a catalyst for my own.

3. I get great ideas by thumbing through magazines. Article titles are usually designed to catch your eye and hook your attention. That is what I want for my titles.

4. A dictionary and a thesaurus are great resources for ideas. Verbs are especially hot in titles.

5. I like going to a music store and checking out album covers and song titles. I also get a lot of good art and graphic ideas.

6. Believe it or not, I get some good ideas by looking at television and movie titles in the *TV Guide*. Okay, I'm getting a little desperate.

7. Rhyming is fun. A good resource for your library is a book on words that rhyme.

8. Great titles can come from acronyms. This is where you create words that begin with the same letter as the lead word. Examples: STEVE . . . **S**teve **T**hinks **E**verything's **V**ery **E**xcellent; DARRELL . . . **D**ashing, **A**wesome, **R**ighteous, **R**iveting, **E**arnest, **L**ovable, **L**ies about himself in acronyms. Okay, a little off-the-wall, but it's *our* book.

9. You can take pretty plain titles and

jazz them up by writing them in unique ways. The visual impact of reading the title catches your attention.

10. You could just rip off your pastor's old sermon titles. No one would probably remember them anyway (heh, heh . . . that's a joke, guys).

CHOOSING TEACHING TOPICS

Obviously, our teaching should be geared toward the needs of the kids we're teaching. Although Scripture can stand alone (God can use any passage to teach truth), special topics are best served when they address specific needs. In Chapter One, I talked about creating a survey to understand needs—a great way of coming up with teaching topics! A survey could ask kids which topics, issues, or subjects interest them. A survey could also list a number of topics and invite kids to mark (or rank) the ones they'd like to discuss.

Any topic should be open to discussion in the church's junior high group. Where else can they hear the good news of God's involvement in their lives? It is up to the wise youth worker to channel controversial issues through his or her "wisdom filter." It's also important to "junior highize" those same issues.

Having a little trouble coming up with some hot topics to program around? No problem. I believe in your ability to do it, but if you are struggling, lost your thesaurus and *TV Guide*, gone into brain lock, or can only come up with topics such as organic gardening and great American rivers, here are 562 hot (some not) ideas that you might be able to build upon . . . from A to Z!

A

abortion
absolutes
abstinence
abundance
abuse
acceptance
accountability
adoption
adultery
adventure
adversity
advertisements
advice
affirmation
affluence
age to start dating
aggression
AIDS
alcohol
aloneness
ambition
angels
anger
anorexia nervosa
anxiety
apathy
apologetics
arguments
athletics
atomic bombs
attitudes
awe of God

B

bad habits
barbs
bashfulness
beatings
beauty
behavior
being
belief
belonging
Bible study
bitterness
blame
boasting
boldness
boredom
born again
boyfriends
breaking up
broken homes
broken promises
brokenness
brothers
building bridges
bulimia
bullies
bummers

busyness

C

cable television
calm
care-giving
celebration
censorship
change
character
cheating
cheerfulness
choices
choosing friends
chores
Christian music
Christmas
church dropouts
cliques
clothes
commercials
commitment
communication
community service
compassion
competition
complacency
complexion
compromise
conduct
confidence
conflict
conformity
confrontation
conscience
consequences
control
controversy
conversations
cooperation
copyright laws
corruption
couch potatoes

country
courage
creation
credibility
crime
criticism
crying
cults
cussing

D

dancing
danger
dares
dating
death
deceit
decency
decision
dedication
defeat
defiance
demons
depression
desires
devotion
dignity
diligence
diplomacy
disasters
discipleship
discipline
discouragement
discrimination
disorientation
divorce
doctrine
doing
double-mindedness
doubt
dreams
drugs
drunkenness

E

Easter
eating disorders
ecology
economy
ego
elderly
embarrassment
emotions
empathy
emptiness
encouragement
endurance
enthusiasm
environment
eroticism
escapism
eternity
ethnocentrism
euthanasia
evangelism
everlasting life
evil
excellence
exclusiveness
excuses
exhortation
expectations

F

failure
faith
faithfulness
falling in love
family
famine
fantasy games
fathers
favoritism
fear
feelings
feminism

fighting
finger pointing
fitting in
flirting
following
foolishness
forgiveness
foundations
frazzled
freedom
French kissing
friends
frustrations
future

G

gangs
getting high
gifts
girlfriends
giving in
global issues
glory
glue sniffing
goals
God's call
godliness
going steady
goodness
goofing off
gore
gossip
GPA
grace
grades
graffiti
grandparents
gratefulness
greed
grief
growing up
grudges
guilt

guns

H

handicaps
hangouts
happiness
hardship
harmony
hassles
hate
healing
healthy habits
heaven
heavy metal music
hell
helping
heroes
high school
holiness
Holy Spirit
home
homeless
homework
homosexuality
hope
hormones
hospitality
hot-tempered
humility
hunger
hurt
hygiene
hypocrites

I

idleness
idols
immigration
immorality
impact
impatience
incest

independence
inferiority
initiative
inner city
innocence
insecurity
insight
insults
integrity
intensity
involvement
isolation

J

jabber
jealousy
Jehovah's Witnesses
jerks
Jesus
Jewish
jitters
joy
judgment
justice
justification

K

killing
kindness
kissing
KKK
know-it-alls
knowledge

L

labels
latchkey kids
laughter
law
laziness
leadership

learning
lifestyle
like-mindedness
listening
loneliness
looks
lordship
losing
love
loyalty
lust
luxury
lying
lyrics of songs

M

mail
making a difference
making out
manipulation
manners
marriage
masks
masturbation
materialism
maturity
me-ism
mealtimes
meekness
mercy
mind control
miracles
missions
misunderstanding
Monday mornings
money
moods
morality
Mormons
mothers
motivation
mourning
mouth

movies
moving
murder
music

N

narcotics
nationalism
needs
negativism
neglect
nerds
neutrality
new life
newborn rights
news
nitty-gritty
nonviolence
normality
nuclear war
nurturing

O

obedience
obstacles
occult
older friends
opinion
opportunities
opposition
optimism
options
order
outcasts
outreach
outsiders
outstretched arms
overcoming

P

pacifism

pain
partying
patience
patriotism
peace
peacemaker
peer pressure
perfection
performance
persecution
perseverance
personal growth
personality clashes
pessimism
petting
popularity
pornography
possessions
possessiveness
potential
poverty
power of God
praise
prayer
pregnancy
prejudice
pride
priorities
privacy
procrastination
promises of God
promises to God
prophesy
prostitution
puberty
punishment
purity
put-downs

Q

quality
quarreling
questions

quests
quick-tempered
quiet times

R

R-rated movies
rationalization
reality
rebellion
reckoning
rejection
relationships
reliability
relief
repentance
reputation
resentment
respect
responsibility
rest
restraint
resurrection
revival
risk
rock and roll
romance
roots
rules
rumors

S

sacrifice
sadness
salvation
sanctuary
Satan
school
secrets
self-esteem
self-hate
self-love
selfishness

sensitivity
servanthood
sex
sexual jokes
shoplifting
shyness
sickness
simplicity
sin
single-mindedness
skepticism
smart alecks
smoking
sorrow
spiritual gifts
standards
stealing
stepparents
strength
stress
strife
struggles
stumbling
style
success
suffering
suicide
support
surprises
suspicion
swearing
sympathy

T

teachers
teamwork
tearing down walls
teasing
telephone
television
temptation
tenacity
tenderness

terrorism
tests
Thanksgiving
thought life
time management
tithing
tomorrows
tongue
transition
treasures
trends
trials
triumphs
trust
truth
TV evangelists

U

ulterior motives
unchaperoned party
unchurched
unconditional love
underachievement
understanding
uniqueness
unity
urban life

V

value
values
vandalism
vanity
venereal disease
vengeance
vices
victory
video games
video movies
violence
virginity
virtue

vision
volunteering
vulgarity
vulnerability

W

war
weakness
weariness
weekends
weight loss
wholeheartedness
why
wickedness
winning

wisdom
witnessing
wonder
work
world view
worry
worship
worth
worthlessness
wounded

X

Xanthippe
xenophobia

Y

yahoos
yawp
yearnings
yesterdays
younger brothers
younger sisters

Z

zealousness
zest for life
Zionism
zits
zzzzz's

ENDNOTES

1. Bill McNabb and Steven Mabry, *Teaching the Bible Creatively: How to Awaken Your Kids to Scripture* (Grand Rapids: YS/Zondervan, 1990).

CHAPTER FIVE

HURDLING THE ROADBLOCKS OF CREATIVE PROGRAMMING

By STEVE DICKIE

Daydreaming is a favorite pastime of mine. Here's a dream that I like to play over and over again in my mind: There's eight seconds left to play in the NBA finals and 50,000 wild-eyed people are screaming in the stands. The score is tied and there's a major problem—the star player on my favorite team has just fouled out of the game. Not to worry. I leave the stands, walk onto the floor, and volunteer to take his place. "Give him the ball," says the coach, "That's Steve Dickie. He'll put it in." The crowd chants my name, "DICKIE, DICKIE." I flash a smile, twinkle my eye, nod to the referee, and confidently state, "Let's play ball." They toss me the ball on the inbounds and I head up the court. All the players clear out of the way. It's me, "Doctor D," one-on-one with the all-star player for the opposing team. I fake right and reverse pivot left. The crowd chants, "Five, four, three, two . . ." With uncanny ability, amazing dexterity, and unequaled style (hey, it's my daydream), I release a high arching thirty footer. As the ball leaves my hand, I'm fouled so hard that I'm sent flying into the stands (I land in the arms of my beautiful wife, of course). Just as I'm about to pass out, I hear a "swish," the buzzer, the announcer scream, "It's goooooooooood," and the roar of the fans. I look into the eyes of my wife (she gazes back with a "you are so wonderful" look). The background music picks up, the houselights dim, and one solitary spotlight is left shining on the two of us. I slowly close my eyes and whisper, "Did I make it?" Cut. . . .

Wouldn't it be great if ministry life was like that, and you always came out a hero? Everything you did, every idea you came up with, and every program you created would be cheered like a winning World Series team in a ticker tape parade. Kids would love you, parents would applaud you, and your church would embrace you. I learned quickly that it doesn't always work out that way.

Programming for junior high ministry isn't always a bed of roses. You would think our efforts would be welcomed and our attempts at creativity would be praised. It often brings the opposite. Creativity does something that many people are not quite willing to accept—it rewrites the rules. It changes the status quo, the norm, and the "way it's always been done." This isn't always appreciated. Many people would just as soon stick with the old way than adjust to any new direction.

To be honest with you, your attempts at creative programming won't always be easy. Although the rewards will be great and the blessings will be many, you will encounter a few roadblocks along the way.

Some roadblocks can be avoided if we know they're there and we keep our eyes open. An alert junior high worker can spot them and steer clear. In his book *Be the Leader You Were Meant to Be,*[1] LeRoy Eims describes this type of roadblock by comparing it to an encounter with a rattlesnake.

One advantage in dealing with these snakes is that they don't try to trick you. When they shake their rattles and show you their fangs, you know what you're up against.

Although some pitfalls of creative programming can be avoided, many frustrations can't. They come with the territory, and we should expect them. Although they will battle us and try to steal away our joy, they can be dealt with when we realize they're there. Here's a look at some of these roadblocks and a few hints on how we can take steps (and leaps) to hurdle them.

TRADITION

Another youth pastor once said to me, "Before you ever think about starting up a new program, think first about how to eliminate the old one." That's a lot easier said than done. Some church programs never die, they just live on forever.

Incredible as it seems, some groups will cling to old programs just because "it's the way it's always been done." Even though the old programs may be lousy programs, they remain as a memorial to something past. Try to shoot them dead or even give them a revitalizing shot in the arm, and watch the sparks fly!

One youth group I know of just won't accept change. The frustrated youth pastor, a friend of mine, would share how every inventive idea and creative program that he introduced would be met with resistance by the youth leadership group. They always wanted to do the same thing they had done last year. (The same they had done last year was usually the same thing they had done the year before, and the year before, and . . .). The original idea wasn't all that bad, he thought, but wouldn't a change of pace be refreshing?

In his experience, however, my friend did learn an important lesson. While resistance to change can create all sorts of havoc for the creative-minded, it is also important to realize that tradition isn't always bad. It can provide security in the midst of a very insecure world. Given the reality of a fragmenting society, kids need traditions that provide stability and consistency. Youth group programs can provide that. We must take care to offer freshness while still maintaining a healthy appreciation of the past.

I find it wise to introduce major creative change at a pace that isn't shocking. Once we prove that our ideas are valid, people will come alongside our creativity more readily. When we've gained their trust, the doors to creative options begin to open wide.

DISCOURAGEMENT

During one vacation, my wife and I rented a couple of mountain bikes and rode around the beautiful Acadia National Park outside Bar Harbor, Maine. We casually spent the day riding through the park, enjoying the lakes and forests. When we began our ride home, I discovered that we had traveled much farther than I realized. It seemed that each time we rode over a hill, there would be another valley and another hill before us. I was getting worn out and a little discouraged. Each time I would climb to the crest of a hill with excitement and anticipation, I would only head into another valley and another discouragement.

Hills and valleys—sounds a little like ministry, doesn't it? One week you're at the top of the hill: Your creative programs are a success, your group is growing, and your kids are responding. The next week you've plummeted into the valley. The lesson you spent hours on was a dud, your staff leaders forgot to do their assigned tasks, and the kids you normally can count on are causing the biggest problems.

Discouragement. If you have ever tried to be creative in your junior high program, you have felt the emotion. There have probably been times when you come home, sink into a chair and sigh, "I just don't want to do this anymore." You know what? You're normal. We all struggle with the pains of discouragement. Believe me, I face it often.

One of the biggest discouragements junior high workers face is seeing few immediate results of our creative efforts. We can work incredibly hard at coming up with some of the most outrageously creative programs imaginable, only to have them meet a disinterested response. That can really be discouraging. It hurts to work at something so hard and wonder if you're even making a difference. When I face this frustration, I remind myself of the nature of junior high work. We're seed planters. Although our creative efforts may not have an impact now, they could be setting some wonderful unknown things into motion that may not bloom until next year, five years, or even twenty years down the line. Isaiah 55:10, 11 encourages me in this process.

"As the rain and the snow come down from heaven, and do not return to it without watering the earth and making it bud and flourish, so that it yields seed for the sower and bread for the eater, so is my word that goes out from my mouth: It will not return to me empty, but will accomplish what I desire and achieve the purpose for which I sent it."

This passage is an encouragement to junior high workers who are striving to communicate the Good News in a relevant and creative way. God just wants us to be faithful; he's in charge of the results.

Another cause for discouragement is our tendency to compare our abilities to the creative abilities of others. Much of that self-criticism is unfair. There are some people who just seem to have the knack for creativity. Put them in most any situation and they will probably be able to pull off creative programs. They are gifted in this area. On the other hand, I'm convinced that creativity can be grown. There are enough resources available to youth workers to allow anyone to come up with great ideas. Don't be discouraged. Our little book here is crammed full of all sorts of ideas that will get you started—and your kids will think they're all your own!

CRITICISM

Ouch—I don't like criticism. I think I'd rather it just go away; unfortunately, it rarely does. As we think and act creatively, we are taking risks. That same risk taking brings out certain elements of criticism from others. Here are a few explanations.

• **Jealousy:** I know it sounds weird, but some people get jealous of your taking creative risks. I figure when you take risks, you're doing something that many people have only dreamed about. You took the risk that they never had the courage to take.

• **Change:** People get comfortable in the "way it's always been done." Your creativity is going to naturally change that way of thinking.

• **Inconvenience:** Creativity requires that we work just a little harder. Some don't like the extra effort it requires.

• **Different vision:** If the people around you don't share your same creative vision, you might expect some degree of criticism.

• **Target error:** Criticism can be justi-

fied. If you are hearing a lot of it, this should probably send up a red flag. You may need to evaluate whether or not you are aiming at the right needs.

You might hear criticism from a variety of voices. Here are a few of the sources.

KIDS. I try to listen to criticism from my junior highers through two different ears (no, not in one ear and out the other). First, I want to take them seriously. What they have to say is important for me to hear. If I'm truthfully committed to designing creative programs around their needs, then their criticism gives me a window to see if I'm successful or not.

Second, I try to look for the real meaning behind their criticism. Often what they say is actually an attempt to communicate a different message. One of the classic comments that I hear from kids is the phrase "This is booooorrrrring." Although the comment could actually mean the program is indeed boring, it often is communicating something entirely different. It might mean, "I feel insecure because I don't know anyone here." It's important to listen to kids, but don't allow their critique to always change your creative agenda.

PARENTS. Criticism from parents is tough, but you better get used to it. I've been in full-time junior high ministry for a long time, and I have never seen a program, successful or not, that didn't garner some element of criticism from parents.

Outside of a few tough circumstances, much criticism from parents is actually a result of our common love for kids. The problem comes when we look at those kids from different perspectives. While parents only look at the needs of their children, the youth worker looks at the needs of the entire group. They don't always coincide.

Having a successful relationship with parents is essential to any creative program. Junior high kids are still very dependent on their parents. They bring the kids to our programs, they usually pay for the events, and they can keep their kids away from what we are doing if they feel like it. I believe it's important to extend to parents the same creative intensity that we extend to junior highers. A great way to start is by creatively opening up the lines of communication with them. Here are few ideas to help you get going.

CREATIVE WAYS TO COMMUNICATE WITH PARENTS

1. Write a weekly summary of your Sunday school or youth group meeting for parents. Include discussion questions to help integrate what you're teaching into the home.
2. Mail a monthly newsletter to parents. Include information on upcoming events, parenting tips, and other helpful articles.
3. Hold parent meetings to promote your programs.
4. Create a parents' group that meets regularly. Provide speakers and discussion relevant to parenting adolescents.
5. Sponsor a special mom's meeting.
6. Sponsor a special dad's meeting.
7. Print regular announcements to parents in the church newsletter or bulletin.
8. Create a parents' council to act as advisors or liaisons to your staff and to other parents.
9. Telephone parents regularly. After you call the kids, talk with the parents.
10. Visit parents at home or take a parent to lunch.
11. Have a table each Sunday stocked with junior high information.
12. Print a brief biography on yourself and your staff—mail it to parents with photos.
13. Leave a "hotline" on your answering machine with up-to-date information.
14. Invite parents to your youth group meeting. Run the program like a typical program. Don't change a thing. This allows parents to see firsthand what you do.
15. Provide a parents' resource ministry where you have books on parenting and adolescence, tapes, and music for loan.

PASTOR. Lucky for me, I've always worked with senior pastors who believe in junior high ministry. They have always appreciated, understood, and even encouraged my creative antics. During my years at Bel Air Presbyterian Church in Los Angeles, my pastor and boss Donn Moomaw, would always tell me that junior high ministry was one of the most important ministries in the church. Sure, he probably gave the choir director and the nursery attendants the same kind of encouragement, but it sure meant a lot to me. I needed to hear it.

When we do receive criticism from our pastors, it's often due to a couple of reasons. First, when they hear criticism about your programs, it is usually from one or perhaps a few sources. What you're doing may be fine and is being received with high marks from the majority, but your pastor is hearing only from a few. Second, your pastor doesn't walk in your junior high shoes. He doesn't necessarily understand the "why" behind some of the creative things you try.

In both instances, communication is once again the key element. I make a habit of sending my senior pastor notes about what we're doing. I also send him a copy of almost every item we print. I discovered long ago that much of a pastor's criticism stems from simply not knowing what's going on. When I am open with him and provide insight as to "why" I do things, he is much more willing to bend with my creativity. Try outlining the process of how you come up with your ideas for your pastor. You might also get into some intentional conversations about creativity with your pastor. This will give you an opportunity to let him come alongside your style.

FAILURE

Here's a bottom line statement: If you are willing to take the risk of being creative in your programs, you are going to occasionally fail. But take note of a second bottom line statement: Failure does not mean you are a lousy youth worker.

A junior high friend recently gave me some wise advice about failure. During a youth group ski trip in the Sierra Nevada Mountains, I skied a lot of runs with Jonathan. A fairly new skier, Jonathan fell many times throughout the day. Some of his crashes were amazing, but each time he'd get back up, brush himself off, and head back down the slope. His philosophy, he told everyone that evening at the lodge, was this: "If you're not falling, you're not learning." Jonathan was right. Failure is a normal part of becoming good at something—creative programming included.

I certainly have had my fair share of failures throughout my ministry. Although some were results of simple goof-ups or Steve Dickie error, many resulted even though I had done everything right. Either way, it isn't necessarily a pleasant feeling. Failure hurts. I recently gave a talk for our junior highers called "If Failure Helps Me Grow, Then Why Do I Feel So Rotten?" I think that describes it well. We know that failure helps build better people, but it still can be pretty disheartening. The good news is that though we may receive ridicule from the world (and even our churches) as a result of failure, Jesus gives us plenty of room to mess up. It's not that he necessarily loves failure; he just loves people who have failed. Brokenness turns us toward God. In the nature of ministry, there is really no better place to be.

It helps to remember that the smartest and most creative people around have encountered failure (that's often the reason why they're so smart and creative). Believe me, you are not alone. There is comfort in that. These people have been slammed, jammed, mashed, and trashed, but never broken. They have discovered that success can be remeasured. Although you can't control results, you can control process. Grab a copy of *When Smart People Fail* by Carole Hyatt and Linda Gottlieb.[2] This book was a major encouragement during one of my life's toughest failures.

FACILITY

I have to admit a sin. Yes, it's a secret sin that is shared by youth workers everywhere: I lust after gymnasiums. If you don't have one, you know what I'm talking about. Anyone want to start a support group?

Awesome facilities are great, aren't they? Who wouldn't want a gym, a youth room, or even a new set of chairs? Reality, however, proves to be a lot different. Most of us have to beg, borrow, or come up with pretty creative alternatives just for a place to meet. We have the enthusiasm for creative programs, we just don't have a great facility.

Good news! You don't have to have a great facility to pull off creative meetings and activities. You get to use your creativity to come up with options. This is the fun part.

Some of my ministry friends choose to hold most of their junior high group meetings in homes. They enjoy such benefits that a home can provide.

—Homes are comfortable and non-threatening.

—Homes are usually in a neighborhood close to the students.

—Homes are usually nice and well kept.

—Homes have great recreational options (swimming pool, table tennis, and so on).

—Homes have food-producing kitchens.

On the other hand, I hold most of our meetings at the church. The room in which we meet is not exactly functional for youth meetings (actually, it's pretty lousy), but we make the best of it. Each Tuesday night, I spend hours "junior highizing" the room. I go to extreme measures to give the room a fun, upbeat, and visible junior high feel. It's a lot of work (especially the teardown), but it helps me turn the facility into a youth-type room. Here are a few suggestions on things that you can try.

CREATIVE WAYS TO ENHANCE A FACILITY

1. Hang banners, signs, or posters.
2. Take photos of your group. Enlarge them and hang on the wall.
3. Create a bulletin board filled with photos, flyers, and upcoming events announcements.
4. Rearrange the chairs into a different formation each week.
5. Play upbeat music as kids arrive.
6. Have a video on screen as kids arrive.
7. Create school banners with the names of your kids' schools on them, and hang them on the wall.
8. Set up a table in your room stocked with flyers about your ministry.
9. Decorate your room to a different theme each week.
10. Set up inexpensive board or table games throughout your room.
11. Provide snacks as the kids arrive (or as they leave).
12. Have a soda machine or video game company place a machine in your room.
13. Paint, wallpaper, or design graphics on the walls.
14. Using duct tape, create a four-square court on the floor.
15. Collect old pillows or seat cushions, and throw them on the floor for kids to sit on.
16. Gather old sofas, chairs, and other furniture to create a lounge area.
17. Frequent auctions and garage sales. You can pick up all sorts of stuff to add to your youth room.

Here's a tip: Go to extremes to clean up after using the church facilities (yes, I'm telling you to clean up your room; now go brush your teeth). I have discovered that many church people base their opinions of your junior high ministry not by changed lives or spiritual growth, but by the shape in which you leave a room after you use it. Because adults often assume that junior highers destroy anything near them (naaaaahhhhh . . .), I will always make sure a room is cleaner when I leave than it was when I found it. Reputation is important in this case. Also, build a positive relationship with your custodians. I think they are secretly the most powerful people in the church. Let them in on your creative process so they understand why you do what you do. You want to have them on your side.

BUDGET

While shopping for a car recently, I quickly learned that there is a big difference between what I want and what I can afford. I should have figured it; just about everything requires money.

It isn't really any different with creative programming. It seems the more creative we get, the more money we need. That leaves us with two scenarios. One, if we have the budget to support our dreams, we don't have to worry about it (that's nice). Two, if we don't have the budget, we can either forget about it, or we can go buy it ourselves (that's tough).

Obviously, we can do a lot without a significant budget. It has been proven over and over again in youth ministries across the country. Usually born out of necessity (isn't that the mother of all invention?), some very creative programs have resulted. God is not limited by money. The good news is that he can do anything he wants.

Just as I mentioned in the comments regarding facilities, the lack of funds is a great opportunity to use your creative powers. There are countless fund-raising options available to you. Try contacting a local school, a Boy or Girl Scout troop, or a service organization. They can steer you toward countless ideas, and they can probably tell you which ones worked and which ones didn't work in your community. I especially like servant sales. People "hire" your students to do a task (clean the garage, mow the lawn, and so on), and then they pay the church the wage. The congregation benefits, the students learn to be servants, and you raise some nice coin.

A TOOL YOU CAN USE

This little tool (found on p. 66) will help you identify your roadblocks and come up with resources to hurdle them. Whenever I come up with a program idea (an event, a retreat, an activity), I use this process. Be sure to check out Chapter Three where Darrell explains the concept of storyboarding.

THE BIG IDEA. To start, I simply write out my idea. For example, this could be a community outreach event, a special anti-drug parents night, or perhaps a prayer night. I write these big ideas on a dry erase board I keep on my office wall. This helps keep them in front of me so I can be thinking them through.

SUPPORTING IDEAS. I then list many ideas that would frame and support my big idea. The bulk of my most creative brainstorming is done here. I hold nothing back—every idea is worth consideration.

ROADBLOCKS. Next, I list out every possible obstacle that could get in my way and keep me from pulling off my big idea. Bluntly honest and very realistic, I include attitudes, people, facility, budget limitations, calendar conflicts, and the like.

HURDLES. After listing all the foreseeable roadblocks, I then list out the resources at my disposal to hurdle each roadblock. Once again, I am detailed in thinking of all possible options.

THEREFORES. At this point, I list goals to use my resources. I also set timelines, due dates, and delegation assignments in this section.

A FEW FINAL WORDS

Be assured your creative efforts will meet plenty of obstacles. Those roadblocks, however, don't have to stop you from succeeding. As a young Christian, I was given some wise advice by a friend. "When you know you're going to encounter a tough situation," he said, "you can gear up for it and let the stretching shape you into a better person. If you aren't watching for it, however, it can sneak up on you and knock you out." I have never forgotten those words. James 1:2–4 says it, too.

Consider it pure joy, my brothers, whenever you face trials of many kinds, because you know that the test-ing of your faith develops persever-ance. Perseverance must finish its work so that you may be mature and complete, not lacking anything.

Stepping into creativity is risky, but the rewards far outweigh the frustrations. It is often just a matter of how we look at the situation. Director Peter Schifter said it well: "There are really two kinds of failure: passive failure—not daring to risk at all, which is criminal; and active failure, which is noble."[3] Don't give up, my friend. Keep on testing your creative wings. Some of your greatest creative successes are still to come!

ENDNOTES

1. LeRoy Eims, *Be the Leader You Were Meant to Be* (Wheaton, Ill.: Victor, 1975), 105.
2. Carole Hyatt and Linda Gottlieb, *When Smart People Fail* (New York: Penguin Books, 1987).
3. Peter Schifter, as quoted in Hyatt and Gottlieb.

ROADBLOCKS TO RESOURCES

THE BIG IDEA: _____

SUPPORTING IDEAS:

1.
2.
3.
4.
5.

6.
7.
8.
9.
10.

ROADBLOCKS:

1.
2.
3.
4.
5.

6.
7.
8.
9.
10.

HURDLES:

1.
2.
3.
4.
5.

6.
7.
8.
9.
10.

THEREFORES:

1.
2.
3.
4.
5.

6.
7.
8.
9.
10.

NOTES AND COMMENTS:

SECTION TWO:
TAKING THE PLUNGE–
PULLING OFF CREATIVE
PROGRAMMING

CHAPTER SIX

CREATIVE IDEAS FOR SUNDAY SCHOOL

By Darrell Pearson

Thirty minutes after the Sunday school class hour was over, Don found me in the hall. His wife, Cathy, was one of my eighth grade teachers. Don informed me that Cathy was still in her classroom, no students in sight, and was unwilling to emerge. Don told me that since it was my program, it was my job to get her out. I went.

Cathy had experienced one of those mornings when everything had gone wrong. The eighth grade boys in her group were in a particularly witty mood, making funny comments about Jesus' life that slowly ate Cathy up. Halfway through her class time, she threw them out and told them she was done teaching. She had lost control as well as her temper, and she wasn't sure what to do except to cry in the empty room. I began to think about a career in real estate.

Sound like your junior high Sunday school sometimes? Maybe it was you or one of your volunteers, but all of us struggle with how to make that sometimes "weakly" hour meaningful to the kids. Here are some ideas on how to make it happen creatively enough to engage the students' interest. It might help when you have to rescue your teachers from the blackhole classroom!

CREATIVE BIBLE TEACHING

The basic problem with so many Sunday morning lessons is that they're so—well, boring. That's a very strange thing to happen, what with the Bible being so full of interesting, provocative, and challenging stories and ideas. But it takes a little creativity to see what Scripture has to offer junior highers.

As you study a Scripture passage, try to imagine that the story involves real people, since it did! Junior highers have a hard time relating to incidents that happened to anybody besides themselves in the last week, much less situations from 2,000 years ago. The Bible must come alive. Picture the story happening in your mind's eye. What's happening that is unusual? Interesting? Funny? What metaphors are being used that kids could visualize?

Take, for example, the story of the man with the withered hand in Luke 6. Imagine the real setting: Jesus in front of the others in the synagogue, especially angering and frustrating the Pharisees. All of a sudden he asks the man with the withered hand to come and stand in front of everyone.

Can you believe the potential for humiliation? The man must have felt like every junior high kid does when he or she gets up in front of the class to do an oral report and people giggle, or the kid that misses the key basket in front of the crowd. Make the setting come alive. These stories really happened, and it is our job to help our students see them as real again. It is also our job to help them see the real Jesus bring wholeness to the people he was around and the people we are around.

To make this story come alive with my group, I acted out the part of the man with the withered hand. A better idea would be to cue someone before your meeting to be ready to stand up in front of the group (an adult might be best because of the nature of the story), then call that person up and "embarrass" him or her before everyone. The healing hand could be dramatically acted out to show the great conclusion to the story.

I have a hard time not seeing humor in almost every passage of Scripture. Could Jesus have not had humor in mind when he talked about a camel going through the needle's eye? What about Aaron telling

Moses that they threw the gold in the fire and out came a calf, or Elijah taunting the pagans that their god must be off relieving himself? The list goes on and on.

When the passage is not humorous, it is still real. Too often we gloss over these passages and don't attempt to see the truth in what is happening.

I recently saw Max McLean's theatrical performance in which he acts out the complete gospel of Mark word for word. The passage in which John the Baptist is beheaded after a young girl's dance had never seemed real to me until this performance. It was unbelievable to encounter the reality of this story through a dramatic presentation. (Don't worry; he doesn't act out the beheading!) We must make the Bible become alive again. Do whatever it takes to help your students see that real people were involved with ancient Scripture. Try the following:

1. Dress up as the biblical character that you are teaching about (hard to do if you're focused on Balaam's donkey, but interesting!).

2. Use a visual aid. For example, if you are talking about James's discussion of the tongue, bring a cow's tongue and use it to illustrate the lesson. Light it on fire if talking about Pentecost.

3. Role-play or make the story into a skit using the students themselves. Write a melodrama in which students act out props as well as characters.

4. Do something totally unrelated to the lesson to get the kids guessing or to wake them up. Hang a camera around your neck at the start of the class; just leave it there the whole time (they'll go nuts trying to figure

out what you're doing), or stop once in a while and take pictures of the group.

5. Play the devil's advocate. Argue against the standard biblical answer and make the kids think. Build them a tough faith by your exploration of the threatening questions.

Okay, it's time to see what you can creatively glean from Scripture. Read Mark 10:46–52 and answer the questions that follow.

Then they came to Jericho. As Jesus and his disciples, together with a large crowd, were leaving the city, a blind man, Bartimaeus (that is, the Son of Timaeus), was sitting by the roadside begging. When he heard that it was Jesus of Nazareth, he began to shout, "Jesus, Son of David, have mercy on me!" Many rebuked him and told him to be quiet, but he shouted all the more, "Son of David, have mercy on me!" Jesus stopped and said, "Call him." So they called to the blind man, "Cheer up! On your feet! He's calling you." Throwing his cloak aside, he jumped to his feet and came to Jesus. "What do you want me to do for you?" Jesus asked him. The blind man said, "Rabbi, I want to see." "Go," said Jesus, "your faith has healed you." Immediately he received his sight and followed Jesus along the road.

1. What is happening in the real setting that might be missing from a casual reading?
2. Who are the characters involved? What might they be like as real people?
3. How might you creatively teach this passage? What would be stimulating and thought provoking?

HOOK, BOOK, LOOK, TOOK

Most of us use published curricula to do our lessons. We may be required to follow a curriculum that our churches or educational committees have determined is most appropriate for our kids, or we may have the freedom to choose materials ourselves. Regardless, you can adapt these resources to work better—or you can write your own material—by following the Hook, Book, Look, Took outline. One of my Sunday school teachers taught this to me years ago, and I have found it very helpful.

HOOK. The opening that grabs the kids' attention, this can be a game, an article from the newspaper, a story, or a song; anything that might grab their interest. It doesn't have to be long, just interesting. Let's say our lesson is on Jesus' words from the Sermon on the Mount concerning God giving good gifts to his children (Matthew 7:7–12).

"Ask and it will be given to you; seek and you will find; knock and the door will be opened to you. For everyone who asks receives; he who seeks finds; and to him who knocks, the door will be opened. Which of you, if his son asks for bread, will give him a stone? Or if he asks for a fish, will give him a snake? If you, then, though you are evil, know how to give good gifts to your children, how much more will your Father in heaven give good gifts to those who ask him! So in everything, do to others what you would have them do to you, for this sums up the Law and the Prophets."

The hook might be bringing rocks into class in a doughnut box. When the top comes off, it's an obvious letdown. Would God do this to us? I once introduced this passage by having my three-year-old daughter unwrap a present from me (it was a stone). Her natural reaction drove the point home well. You might simply bring the nicest gift you have ever received from anyone and show it to the group, describing what it means to you.

BOOK. Here you simply read and study the Scripture passage. You get creative by using a variety of versions or by having different kids read it emphasizing certain words. You might try a Bible game, such as a crossword puzzle based on the passage.

LOOK. Try to determine what the passage is trying to say (not what you want it to mean). You might have to talk about the role of a good father, since many kids probably don't have one. The goal of this step is to accurately determine what the writer—or Jesus—meant to convey.

TOOK. Now you apply the passage. What does the passage mean for junior highers in their lives? How can they go away living their lives a bit differently? Since the passage concludes with the Golden Rule, it might be a good application to talk about what that means for kids today. In what situations is it hardest for them to treat others well? Your application might have them write notes to their siblings apologizing for past tortures or committing themselves to cease starting fights during basketball practice.

Hook, book, look, took: It's simple, but it works! The following lesson plan outline is based on these ideas. Copy it and use it to plan your lessons.

TOPIC:

PASSAGE:

MAIN IDEA OR POINT I AM TRYING TO COMMUNICATE:

Hook:

Book:

Look:

Took:

CONCLUSION: (Have I made the application clear?)

STUFF I NEED FOR THIS LESSON:

STRUCTURING THE TIME AND THE CLASS

It's no secret that it's tough for a lot of junior highers to stay with one thought or concept for more than a few minutes. Structure your time well so that the class flows smoothly and quickly from one angle to the next. It's a good rule of thumb to focus on one project or idea for five to ten minutes maximum. The only time this may vary is when the kids, by virtue of an issue or concern they are dealing with, have forced a new topic on you. It's quite possible then to spend forty-five minutes talking about this one particular issue.

Since you never really know exactly how long an activity will take, plan to have an idea or two to fill time when necessary. When I was in the eighth grade, I had a substitute science teacher whose carefully planned lecture lasted about ten minutes. He had planned on questions and answers for the remaining thirty minutes, but when there were no questions . . . well, let's just say it was a very long thirty minutes. Keep something up your sleeve to pull out when the need arises, or simply be prepared to dig into a topic or Scripture in more detail if the kids are up for it.

There are lots of opinions about how to structure class size and makeup. You can have one class for all the junior highers (never have a combined junior/senior high class, no matter what the size is—unless the senior highers are teaching assistants), or you can break down by grade or sex. The makeup of each individual group is the main determining factor concerning how classes are structured. Sometimes a chatty class of six is harder to teach than a quiet class of twenty. What are your kids like? If you have the size to break up into groups, keep some balance with leaders and followers, talkers and listeners, thinkers and doers. The creative part comes in when it all starts to seem boring. Then, be ready to switch gears: Combine classes for a special presentation or discussion, take a field trip and meet someplace else, or offer a reward for the class's interest and involvement in the lessons.

DISCIPLINE

How do you creatively control your class—at least enough so that something is communicated? Here are a few suggestions.

1. Keep in mind that nobody has total control over any group of junior highers! There is always an element of unruliness that is inherent in the species. If you meet someone who has complete control, he or she probably has either very bored students or no students at all.

2. Whenever possible, attack your discipline issues in an individual manner. Yelling at kids in front of their peers doesn't work. Sometimes it means removing a student from the others and talking one-on-one with him or her. I have found that approaching the person outside of the morning lesson time is best. Going out for ice cream or a Coke and talking about your need for her or his support can be very effective. Many of my volunteer teachers have found that allowing the problem person the chance to help teach is effective (often the person is bored and needs a different challenge). Giving the child a small assignment and helping him or her work on it during the week takes time, but it cures the problem.

3. Take the positive approach whenever possible. A few years ago, a best-selling book entitled *The One-Minute Manager* offered some good advice that I have appreciated ever since. The quote was "Help people reach their full potential—catch them doing something right."[1] Whenever you see the student who always causes problems doing *anything* that's positive, reinforce it! Let the child know you saw it and appreciated it.

4. Remember, behind every discipline problem, there is a real person struggling with real issues. Rarely does a student act up for no reason at all. Try to discover the reason: Is it family? School? Friends? Fitting in? A crisis in the person's life?

CREATIVE PREPARATION

Do you often find yourself in the Saturday night grind—the realization that tomorrow you teach and you have to cram something together tonight? Do yourself a favor: When Sunday morning is over, take a few minutes and look over the topic for next week. Then you have a few days to let it take root and grow.

In her book *Creative Teaching Methods*,[2] Marlene LeFever says there are five steps to getting your lesson ready. First, there is preparation, where you take the time to do the groundwork of studying the Bible and your curriculum thoroughly. Do you know the passage well enough to teach it? Second, there is incubation, the process of letting that Word speak to you personally. As you contemplate the lesson, you start to have thoughts about creative ideas that will make it come alive for your students. Third is illumination, the realization that something significant is happening here. "Eureka!" is the word LeFever uses to describe the experience of illumination. Fourth is elaboration, the writing of the lesson plan. Finally, there is verification, the process of self-evaluation once the lesson has been taught. It doesn't seem that creative to simply look at your lesson a week early, but it leads to creative thinking. Who knows what will happen during the week to stimulate creative ideas for your lesson?

ODDS AND ENDS

The following thoughts, guidelines, and creative ideas are things I have learned over the years to make Sunday school an enjoyable experience.

1. Never use handouts! Junior highers think they're for little kids. Few will ever find their way home, much less into the kids' minds. For the student who likes to read further, mail out something on the subject that is more interesting than take-home papers.

2. Don't flip through page after page of lesson plans—you look unprepared. Copy on one sheet the major thoughts you need so you don't change pages or give the appearance that you're copying from a book.

3. Buy blank slides and pass out pens for the kids to draw on them. In a half hour you can produce a great slide show with a music background that the kids created themselves. This is a great alternative lesson plan that is ready to go anytime it is needed.

4. Put part of your lesson on videotape. Have a conversation between the tape and yourself to teach the lesson.

5. Always evaluate a curriculum by thinking through who *your* students are. Curriculum writers have never met your class.

6. Whenever you can, encourage kids to learn by their own involvement. Get their hands on something that they can shape or write on. Role-play if you know your group well, or have them read a skit together.

7. Puzzles and games are always a hit. Try something from the books *Good Clean Fun*[3] and *Good Clean Fun, Volume 2*[4] by Tom Finley.

8. If you can't seem to find junior high material and curricula that meet your group's needs, try high school material and adapt it slightly. David C. Cook's *Pacesetter* series is a good

example of stuff that works with junior highers.[5]

9. Use visual objects whenever they are mentioned in the passage. Food and junior highers always go together particularly well!

In the story at the beginning of this chapter, I left poor Cathy stuck in the eighth grade classroom. She did recover—in fact, her students called her on the phone that week, asked her to continue teaching, and promised to get their behavior to an acceptable level. She not only finished the year with them, but she taught them all through their ninth grade year as well. Her productive teaching hinged on her willingness to take their crisis as a class and move ahead with it. She was willing to admit that sometimes her class *was* boring and to do something about it. A creative Sunday school doesn't mean everything will always go smoothly, but it does mean you can take a positive approach and respond to that wild junior high behavior with some creative class preparations. Be ready to shock your students with new and creative ideas. After all, they will continually be doing their best to shock you.

ENDNOTES

1. Kenneth Blanchard and Spencer Johnson, *The One-Minute Manager* (New York: William Morrow, 1983), 39.
2. Marlene LeFever, *Creative Teaching Methods: Be An Effective Christian Teacher* (Elgin, Ill.: David C. Cook, 1985).
3. Tom Finley, *Good Clean Fun* (Grand Rapids: YS/Zondervan, 1986).
4. Tom Finley, *Good Clean Fun, Volume 2* (Grand Rapids: YS/Zondervan, 1988).
5. *David C. Cook's Pacesetter* (Elgin, Ill.: David C. Cook, 1986).

CHAPTER SEVEN

CREATIVE WEEKLY MEETINGS

By Steve Dickie

I love Tuesdays. A few years ago, I loved Fridays. Before that, it was Thursdays. Whatever the day of the week, if my youth group met that evening, I loved it. Remember that feeling you'd get as a kid when Christmas was drawing near? When you thought of it, you'd get a wonderful feeling of excitement inside. That's how I feel about our weekly program.

Why is it such a big deal for me? First, it gives me the opportunity to do what I can't do on Sunday mornings. Although Sunday school provides many opportunities, it also has its limitations. The meeting time is often short and early, the clothing is usually dressy, and the atmosphere is sometimes formal. An additional meeting allows me to structure the time in a much different manner.

Second, it gives me a place to unleash my powers of creativity. I tell you, I love creating bizarre games, off-the-wall signs and posters, crazy skits, meaningful discussion questions, unique message titles, and enlightening ways of communicating God's truth. It's fun to create a plan. It's even more fun to watch it come together.

Third, I simply like being with kids. I care about who they are and what they think. Spending time with them is fun for me. I love it when Calley talks nonstop about everything, when Lea tells her dumb jokes, when Michael does his impersonation of me, and when Tim so honestly shares his struggles and frustrations. I like being with them, and I'm pretty sure they like being with me, too.

I'm convinced that you can enjoy your weekly group meeting. You'll love it, your kids will love it, and your kids will love you for it. With the road map of creativity as our guide, let's take a look at how we can head in the right direction.

WHEN TO MEET

DAY OF THE WEEK. Throughout my years as a full-time junior high minister, I have coordinated programs that have met on almost every day of the week. Frankly, I'm not convinced that any day is necessarily the "right" day for a weekly program. A detailed examination of the needs of your area is the only way to determine what is best.

During my first five years of junior high ministry, our weekly program met on Friday nights. It was very successful and met many needs among the kids, the parents, and the community. At my current church, however, a Friday night program would have great difficulty. The needs of the junior high world we're dealing with is entirely different. Here are a few factors to consider when determining what day is best for your group.

• **Room availability:** If facility space is at a premium, it may determine when you meet. The meeting day of a group I'm currently leading was determined simply by the fact that it was the only day the room was available.

• **Area schedule:** It is best to avoid direct competition with other community or school events that would draw junior highers. Of course, if some events are offering a negative influence, you may want to schedule your program as a creative alternative.

• **Tests and homework:** A little research might show what days most students receive the bulk of their assignments and tests. Certain nights might be big "study" nights.

• **Parents' schedules:** Junior high kids are dependent on their parents for transportation to meetings. A wise youth worker is sensitive to parents' schedules.

• **Sibling events:** Many churches try to schedule youth events (elementary, children, high school) on the same evening—separate programs, but the same night. This helps parents who have children of different ages from making multiple trips.

TIME OF THE DAY. Once again, needs would determine the best time of day to meet. Here are a few considerations that might help to determine that time.

• **Traffic:** If you live in an area where there is heavy traffic, it's important to consider how difficult it is to get to your meeting site.

• **Parents' work:** If one or both parents work, they may be juggling a tough timetable when coming home from work, making dinner, getting other siblings to activities, and so on. Be extra sensitive to single parents.

• **Special interest activities:** After-school activities, such as sports, plays, music, and dancing can create scheduling conflicts. Often such conflicts are seasonal (for example, football in the fall).

• **Homework:** Although some kids would prefer to forget about it, their parents usually want homework done before any outside activities. This is especially tough when they are also involved with an after-school activity.

• **Staff schedules:** When are your volunteer staff leaders available? Their schedules might determine a meeting time.

• **Other church programs:** Some groups wrap other programs around their weekly meetings (choir, small groups, sport leagues). It's often smart to combine these programs (Choir: 5:00–6:00 p.m.; Dinner: 6:00–6:30 p.m.; Meeting: 6:30–8:00 p.m.).

WHERE TO MEET

Last year I went to a memorial service for

a dear friend. No, nobody had died. I had come to witness the tearing down of a building I had known as the Youth Center during my first years of ministry. Although the old center was being razed for the development of a beautiful new youth facility, I still couldn't help but recall the wonderful experiences that were part of that old building. It had spoiled me. It had a large auditorium, a full stage, a complete sound and lighting system, a kitchen, a conference room, a book and tape library, an arts and craft room, a darkroom, a projection room, and a number of small to midsize meeting rooms. We even had a lighted basketball court, sand volleyball, shuffleboard, and a gas fire ring outside. What a great place to hold a program.

I have discovered reality since leaving that facility. As many of us know, a multifunctional building can be nothing more than a dream in youth worker heaven. It is tough enough to find a decent room with chairs that aren't bent or broken. Quite a few of us are desperately looking for a place that our group of kids can call "home."

The most common places to meet are in homes or at the church itself. Both have advantages and disadvantages. Although homes have kitchens (with food!), comfortable furniture, and soft carpets, homes can also have kids and pets that cause distractions, rooms too small for wild games, and locations that are occasionally out of the way.

Churches provide a location known to all, room to run around, the absence of fear that you'll damage someone's house, and easy access to your office and supplies. On the other hand, a church can be a fearful place to unchurched kids and parents and an unfriendly environment if your meeting room is poor.

If either of these places is unavailable or inadequate, we can use our creativity to come up with some options. Here are a few that you might consider.

CREATIVE PLACES TO HOLD A MEETING

1. Meet in a city or a community building.
2. Many shopping centers, banks, and stores have meeting rooms that are available to the public.
3. Club, lodge, or community organizations (American Legion, Elks, women's or senior citizen clubs) might have a room available.
4. Meet at the Y or the boys' or girls' club (many have gyms).
5. Meet outside (weather permitting). Parks are great for summer meetings.
6. Meet in a barn.
7. Try school facilities. If the public schools prohibit church use, try private schools.
8. If there's a college in your town, inquire about the use of its rooms. Don't overlook business, trade, or real estate schools.
9. Many restaurants have meeting rooms available.
10. Meet in a warehouse.
11. Many apartment complexes and housing tracts have meeting rooms.
12. See if another church has a room available.
13. Contact the chamber of commerce for options.
14. Contact local businessmen. They might love to open up their buildings to a worthy group.
15. Contact people who coordinate wed-

dings. They may have ideas from their experience in finding reception sites.

16. Try putting a notice in your church bulletin or newsletter appealing for a meeting site. Someone might have a great place for you.

ROOM DYNAMICS

Although content is the prime ingredient of a meeting, it is also important to think through the dynamics that allow content to be received effectively. This includes room dynamics. Youth workers would be wise to spend a fair amount of time setting up their room to be used in the best possible way. The dynamics of a facility are extremely important in communicating effectively.

DISTRACTIONS. Before our weekly meeting, I walk through our room to make sure there is nothing to distract the kids from what I want to happen during the night's program. I carefully determine a "focus center" in the room where I will stand (or sit) to direct the meeting. When it's time for me to have the attention of the group, it is important for all eyes to be able to easily focus on that spot. There should be nothing around or behind me (like a window) that would allow the kids' focus to shift.

TEMPERATURE. A room too hot can put kids to sleep, and a room too cold can be a distraction.

LIGHTING. An adjustment of the room lights can create an important room dynamic. Having the lights up and bright creates a mood of openness and energy. Having the lights down and soft creates a mood of quiet and reflection. I personally like lights bright. I go crazy in dimly lit rooms and am always getting in trouble

for turning on every light in the house (it drives my wife nuts). I like the energy it brings. During a recent meeting at church, I was getting very frustrated with the lethargy of the kids. I later discovered the problem was the room lighting—it was too dark. After the lights were changed, the kids' responses were entirely different.

ROOM SIZE. If you can choose your room size, it's usually best to pick a room that matches the size of your group. A room that's too large can intimidate; a room that's too small can strangle. On the other hand, a large room allows for a lot of activity (games), and a smaller room can create a great level of energy. A large room can be reduced by strategically placing such things as mobile blackboards, projection screens, and large planters at angles to block off large sections of space. It's a great way of turning a large room into a comfortable space. You can also position lighting in such a way to define space.

SEATING. Depending on what I want to have happen during a meeting, we use chairs or sit on the floor. During non-Sunday school meetings, the kids are usually dressed in a way that is more conducive to sitting on the floor. Eliminating chairs also allows a leader flexibility. You can make a transition quickly from one part of the program to another without the hassle of moving chairs. If you do use chairs, be creative in their arrangement. If you want to lecture to the kids, set up rows. It is much more effective, however, to create a circle or a semicircle. Anything you can do to encourage discussion and participation in your meeting works to your advantage. Arrange the chairs a different way every time you use them. This keeps the kids guessing as to what's coming next. Here's a great little trick: If you have trouble with kids sticking to the back rows, go to the back of the room and say, "Okay, everyone turn your chairs around. This is now the front of the room. Surprise." I like it when they never know what to expect. Another note: If you sing, I have discovered that many junior high groups don't sing well when the chairs are structured in a circle. There seems to be something intimidating about having others see you sing. One final note: Who says we must have a center aisle when we set up chairs? I like to eliminate it by bringing the chairs together. This enables me to focus on one large group instead of two separate groups. If you do have a center aisle, then don't be afraid to walk down it while you're talking to your kids. Move around a lot—it gives your meeting energy!

WHAT TO DO

If you were to spend some time with me, you'd quickly discover my deep love for Mexican food. My favorite is a taco with the works. It has become somewhat of a ritual for me to come home after church on Sunday, head to the kitchen, and build the "Steve Dickie Mucho Grande Taco Especial." After I grate the cheese, shred the lettuce, cut the tomatoes and peppers, and pour the salsa, I slap all those wonderful ingredients into a nice warm tortilla, sit back on the sofa, and munch my heart away.

Putting together a creative program is a lot like building a taco. Although the ingredients are very different, when they are put together a wonderful thing results. Here's a look at some essential "ingredients" that are important to a creative weekly meeting.

SNAP, CRACKLE, AND POP. I love the sound my cereal makes when I pour milk on it. Okay, I'm easily entertained. Anyway, the sound tells me that my cereal is crisp, fresh, and inviting. Yes, I'm stretching this illustration, but I want my meeting to have the same kind of feeling. It should be crisp, fresh, inviting, and full of energy. Chances are the energy is already there. It's my task to capture it and channel it into positive elements. I try to accomplish this by breaking the structure into many small segments. This keeps everything within the kids' attention span. Of course, it's vital to keep things moving quickly between each segment.

AN "OH, BOY!" ATTITUDE. I recently attended a movie with about thirty of my junior highers. Although I wouldn't necessarily say the movie was downright hilarious, I found myself roaring with laughter during many of the scenes. When my kids laughed, it was natural to laugh right along with them. It made a mediocre movie seem like a blockbuster. Enthusiasm is contagious. When we are surrounded by other enthusiastic people, it's easy to join right in.

This is an important ingredient in making your meeting work. Your enthusiasm and "Oh, boy!" attitude will keep a meeting positively paced (even when everything else seems to be failing). It's amazing what my staff has been able to convince the kids to do just because they were enthusiastic about it. Oh, boy!

ATTENTION TO DETAIL. If things can go wrong, they will. When we step into creativity, we are often stepping into untested waters, so take extra efforts to be thorough in planning your meeting. It will help you skirt most disasters. I generally plan for at least one glitch to happen. Don't let these problems get you down too much. I have found that some of my most creative meetings have been the result of my original plans falling apart. Conflict often forces us to take creative risks. We have no other choice.

Before a meeting, I think through alternatives that I can jump into when the inevitable occurs. I keep an "emergency tool kit" in my office for this purpose. The kit, a fishing tackle box, contains such priceless youth worker supplies as masking tape (like gold to a youth leader), chalk, a whistle, overhead pens, marker pens, guitar picks, and a spare projector bulb. The box also contains a couple of ideas for games (a cassette tape of TV theme songs for a trivia game), a list of crazy discussion questions, and a Bible study or two. My tool box has bailed me out of more than a couple tough meetings over the years.

David Veerman, a veteran youth worker and author of *Reaching Kids Before High School*,[1] shares what he calls "Veerman's Laws for Youth Meetings." He's right on target.

VEERMAN'S LAWS FOR YOUTH MEETINGS

1. There will always be a pet in the house that will wander into the room.
2. If there is a TV in the room, it will be turned on.
3. If something can spill, it will.
4. The projector bulb will burn out.
5. The printed announcement will always have an important typo (day, time, place).
6. Half of the kids will not know about the meeting—they didn't get the mailer, get called, or see the

announcement in the bulletin.
7. When you give junior highers a paper to keep, they will lose it in less than ten minutes.
8. Surefire crowd breakers always bomb.
9. When you fill up every minute of your meeting (in your planning), everything will take longer than you expected.
10. When you already have gaps in the meeting (in your planning), everything will go more quickly than you expected.

A PLACE TO BELONG. I recall receiving some very wise advice from one of my mentors during my early years of ministry. "When a kid comes to your meeting," he shared, "make the youth feel like the most important person in the world—just for walking through the door of your room." Sound advice. Kids need to feel like they belong. Your meeting should offer that identity.

A CREATIVE TWIST. One of my all-time favorite movie lines comes from the 1989 hit, *Dead Poets Society*. The scene has a young student flippantly reading a poem he had halfheartedly written as an assignment. "The cat sat on a mat," he stated. The professor's response is wonderful. "There's nothing wrong with being simple," he shares, "but never be ordinary." I love it. I remember when I saw the movie I raised my hand and shouted, "Yes!" loud enough to draw stares from all the other people in the theater. The line teaches us a great truth in programming. Never be ordinary! Your task for creative meetings is to take the simple, the ordinary, the way everyone-else-does-it, and give it just enough of a twist to make it fresh and new. A weekly program dedicated to this concept will surely be a success. Darrell offers some insight into how to develop these creative powers in Chapter Three.

PUTTING IT TOGETHER (A MINISTRY MODEL)

Now that we've taken a look at some of the ingredients for a weekly meeting, let's put it together in a working model. With the understanding that the possible formats are countless, I will offer one as a sample. The sample is modeled after a program that I am currently running in Los Angeles. Believe me, we have struggles and failures just like anyone; I merely offer what we do as a catalyst for thinking through ways to implement a weekly meeting.

Our program meets each Tuesday night, 7:15–9:00 p.m.—we call it "Toozday Night." I spent months trying to come up with a creative, catchy name. Okay, so you think I should keep looking—I still like it. The name is very visual so I can do a lot with it graphically. It's also hard to forget what night of the week we meet. Creating a name for your meeting is smart and can be fun. Try having a contest in which the kids come up with ideas.

Let's walk through a typical "Toozday Night" program and take a limited look at what we do.

JUNIOR HIGH TOOZDAY NIGHT PROGRAM

TOOZDAY NIGHT BASIC PHILOSOPHY

We understand that it is during junior high that many of the core transitions, decisions, and questions of life take place. Therefore, we are committed to creating a program where these core needs can be met. We attempt to achieve this at Toozday Night by focusing on the whole person.

PHYSICALLY. Our program is very upbeat (yes, even wild). Junior highers need a place where they can get their rowdies out. Of course, we must combine the crazy with the gentle.

MENTALLY. We deal with real issues that are relevant to junior highers. Through a variety of media, with an emphasis on discussion, we want to challenge kids to think. We usually deal with topical issues, focusing on the handles that God gives us to deal with our hassles.

SOCIALLY. We want our program to be a place where "everyone knows your name." Through a combination of large group, team group, small group, and individual interaction, we want kids to know that they are significant and capable. It is imperative that they know they can make a difference and can have an impact.

SPIRITUALLY. The rope that consistently runs through our program is the good news of Jesus Christ. We desire junior highers to discover the relevance of Jesus and to begin a personal relationship with him. All games, recreation, events, discussions, talks, and meetings are merely scaffolding to set up this purpose. We can never lose sight of this. Although staff leaders model this through their presence and character, we must be ready to intentionally challenge kids to consider Jesus.

Our Toozday Night program should attempt to break misconceptions that kids have of Christianity by being . . . purposely fresh, consistently relevant, always relational.

PREMEETING. Before the actual meeting takes place, it is important to determine an objective for the meeting. I like to call this the "big idea." Each meeting should have one. While an examination of needs will usually direct me, a few basic questions can help determine the meeting objective. On a piece of paper (or on the dry erase board in my office), I write the following simple words: who, what, where, when, why, and how. I can usually determine my meeting's big idea by answering these questions. I then create activities within the meeting framework to achieve that objective.

Where you position the activities within the program structure is very important. Use the wild stuff at the beginning and move into softer elements later in the meeting. You want the program to flow in such a way that each activity sets up the next activity.

FLOW-IN (7:15–7:30 P.M.). We purposely structure some "hang out" time at the beginning of our meeting. As kids arrive, they talk (sometimes wrestle) with each other and the staff members, play a few spontaneous games we've set up, dance around to the music playing over the sound system, watch a video we have in the corner, or just mingle around the room. The kids love this time (they keep showing up earlier to have more of it). It's great for our staff to meet kids and casually touch base with them.

A table is set up where the kids sign in as they arrive. We have four sign-in sheets: one for first timers, one for second timers, one for third timers, and one for those who have been to the program more than three times. This helps us to know who's there and who's not, to follow up on visitors, and to track our effectiveness of bringing back people for a second, third,

and fourth time.

Here are a couple of my favorite things to do as kids arrive during our flow-in.

• **Wall games:** Pictures of famous people (cut from magazines) are placed on the walls throughout the room. As the kids arrive, they try to guess who the people are. I also put up a variety of other trivia. The possibilities are limitless.

• **Trash can shoot:** I set out a trash can and invite kids to shoot baskets. Kids line up to shoot for distance or to see who can make the most baskets in a row.

• **Four square:** Yes, it's the same game we played as kids. Using duct tape, we frame a court on the floor. The kids line up to play as they arrive. It's not just a little kid's game.

WELCOME AND ANNOUNCEMENTS (7:30–7:40 P.M.). The kids sit down and we kick off the group part of our program at this time. Although our announcements are brief, we attempt to make them as creative as possible. Through the use of creative skits, music, photography, art, and video, the announcement and publicizing of upcoming events can be pretty exciting.

CROWD BREAKER (7:40–7:50 P.M.). A crowd breaker serves as a break into the program. It is ideally used as a way of warming and loosening the group. A wise youth worker will think through a crowd breaker seriously. While the activity can enhance the program, it can also hurt if it's handled without any forethought. Crowd breakers shouldn't threaten, intimidate, embarrass, or model questionable behavior. It is also important that it be used at the right moment in the program's schedule—it should set up or enhance your goal. I have seen many ill-timed crowd breakers ruin a potentially effective meeting. A great resource for crowd breakers is the *Ideas Library*, available from Youth Specialties.[2] This multi-volume collection of great ideas is a must for any youth worker's library.

RECREATION EVENT (7:50–8:10 P.M.). During our program we always schedule a large recreation event. Stay tuned for more on this issue in Chapter Thirteen.

THEME PRESENTATION (8:10–8:20 P.M.). As previously mentioned, each meeting has a specific objective. Using a variety of means, such as music, singing, video, slides, drama, and the like, we work to communicate our big idea. This time helps us focus on that theme. For example, if we are dealing with the topic of getting along with parents, we may present a video that shows interviews of kids at the mall sharing what frustrates them about their moms and dads. We might perform a dramatized vignette of an encounter between a parent and a kid. Pick up the following books for some wonderful ideas on using video and drama: Rick Bundschuh's *101 Outrageous Things to Do With a Video Camera*[3] and *Super Sketches for Youth Ministry* by Debra Poling and Sharon Sherbondy.[4]

TOPIC INPUT (8:20–9:00 P.M.). Everything we have done has been to set up this time—this is what the meeting is all about. Frankly, if it weren't for a junior higher's limited attention span, I would spend the entire meeting dealing with the core stuff. Realistically, however, they need variety.

Although a talk can be an effective tool, I like to use as many styles as possible. A variation in our approach keeps kids guessing *and* interested. Many of these style options are covered in Chapter Four.

FLOW-OUT (9:00–9:10 P.M.). Although our evening ends at 9:00 p.m., I

consider the time immediately following our conclusion to be one of the most important parts of our program. I encourage our staff to use this time to follow-up with the kids regarding our evening's topic. My favorite picture is our staff leaders all over the room talking, sharing, and praying with kids. A few games are also available to help channel the energy of the kids.

POST EVENT. After the meeting is over, I spend the next few days evaluating what went wrong and what went right. I also send out quite a few notes to welcome first timers, to encourage and compliment my staff, and to follow up on various things that kids may have shared. Follow-up is incredibly important. Just as we work hard to set up significant things in our meetings, we need to work just as hard at following up on the results.

SPECIAL EVENT NIGHTS

In all honesty, we don't always work toward a deep, meaningful, or spiritual objective during our weekly meetings. Occasionally we will host some sort of special event during our weekly meeting time frame. These events help give our program a good change of pace that the kids really appreciate.

We usually do about one special night each month. Although we do many events outside our weekly program, we like to do "specials" during the regular Toozday Night hours. The kids already have the night written into their schedules, and it provides a good opportunity for them to get their friends to attend the program. Consequently, we will usually heavily publicize these special nights.

Sometimes the specials are very evangelistic; others are just plain wild, bizarre, and off-the-wall. For some great ideas, I encourage you to pick up a copy of *Creative Socials and Special Events* by Wayne Rice and Mike Yaconelli.[5] Meanwhile, here are a few of my own.

CREATIVE SPECIAL EVENT MEETINGS

1. Build a theme event around an object. Create games, skits, and other fun stuff around such things as toenails, Hawaiian shirts, moose, or event swimming caps. You name it, you can probably build something around it.
2. You can do a lot with decades. Create an event with the 1950s, 1960s, 1970s, or 1980s in mind.
3. Holidays are great times for theme events. How about focusing on some of the minor holidays such as Flag Day, Washington's Birthday, or Groundhog Day? You can even create your own holiday (National Pizza Day; National Bake Steve Dickie Chocolate Chip Cookies Day).
4. Create a meeting around a color. Everyone dresses in red, blue, polka-dot, or camouflage.
5. Focus around a TV show—current favorites or reruns.
6. Try a theme around one of the year's top movies. You might pick out an old classic. Check your local video store for ideas.
7. A popular theme idea is to build an event around food items (pickles, bananas, watermelon—lots of options here).
8. Events based on school are fun. Do a whole meeting around a school subject such as history or math.
9. It's fun to try doing events that are "out of place" on the calendar. How about a Christmas party in July or a heat wave in January?
10. Here are a few other favorites: Break-a-world-record theme; baby theme; cowboy theme; talent show theme; any theme that lets you dress up (surfers, clowns, aliens, construction workers); youth leader imitation event (kids come dressed like you and do impersonations of you—this is fun).

The possibilities here are endless. Have fun exploring the options. Be sure to check out Chapter Four for some "serious" issues to program around.

A FINAL WORD

Just a simple word of advice—enjoy your meeting. Spending time with junior high kids can be fun. Your time with them each week doesn't have to be a dreaded event or a weekly chore. Enjoy it—you can have a blast. Honest!

ENDNOTES

1. David Veerman, *Reaching Kids Before High School* (Wheaton, Ill.: Victor, 1990).
2. *Ideas Library*, Youth Specialties, 1224 Greenfield, El Cajon, CA 92021.
3. Rick Bundschuh, *101 Outrageous Things to Do With a Video Camera* (Ventura, Calif.: Gospel Light/Light Force, 1988).
4. Debra Poling and Sharon Sherbondy, *Super Sketches for Youth Ministry* (Grand Rapids: YS/Zondervan, 1991).
5. Wayne Rice and Mike Yaconelli, *Creative Socials and Special Events* (Grand Rapids: YS/Zondervan, 1986).

CHAPTER EIGHT

CREATIVE CAMPS, TRIPS, AND RETREATS

By Steve Dickie

You can't believe how excited I am about a vacation that Linda and I are taking this year. We will be driving from Southern California to Canada. "Nice, but no big deal," you might say. Let me explain why I'm so excited. Linda has finally agreed to let us spend the whole trip camping. Yes! For years I have wanted her to do this with me. I came close a couple of years ago when she agreed to hike in the Sierra Nevada Mountains with me (even though we had to stay in a motel as our base camp). The big turn around in her attitude came when she started reading my *Outside* magazine. A wonderful journal on outdoor living, the magazine contains some of the most awesome pictures and stories imaginable. Just looking at it makes you yearn for adventure. Well, she's caught the bug and I'm in heaven. We'll send you a postcard.

I love adventure! Camping, trips, exploration, checking out new places . . . what a blast! It's no wonder that I love youth ministry so much. Not only do I get to create some of the most outrageously amazing adventures through camps and retreats, I also get to participate in them. The memories still fill my senses: The thrill of being towed behind a speeding ski boat, the brilliance of a starlit sky, the roaring laughter of a hilarious skit, the wonderful harmony of singing voices, the gentle tears from a changed heart, and a new understanding of a kind and loving God. I have often said that I probably have one of the best jobs in the world, and when I am with my junior highers on a trip, camp, or retreat, I can guarantee it. Let's take a look at this area of ministry and see why I think it's so great. With some wise decision making, a little positive thinking, and a ton of creativity, your camps, trips, and retreats can be the best adventures imaginable.

WHY CAMPS, TRIPS, AND RETREATS?

I am always running into people who were once kids in my youth ministry. Although it makes me feel old, it's really a kick to see them. After a few laughs about some of the crazy things we used to do, I always ask if anything stands out in their memories. Practically everyone points back to our trips. Whether it was summer camp, a weekend retreat, or a ski trip, they all seem to remember a trip as their most memorable moments. "It was such a big deal to get away and go someplace," they share.

Kids love to get away. It's also pretty good for them. In his book *Growing Up in America*, Anthony Campolo shares the following:

> Getting the kids out of their normative environments and away from the identity symbols that weakly prop up their fragile egos can provide a setting where, in the words of the sociologist Peter Berger, an "alteration of consciousness" can occur. On a retreat, removed from the disruptions of TV and the distractions of a typical weekend, junior-high kids can be directed to spiritual things.[1]

Campolo hit the mark. Great ministry can occur when kids get out of their normal environments. Here are a few things I believe can happen.

THEY EXPERIENCE ADVENTURE. Adventure is an excellent learning environment. It allows us to communicate to kids that Christianity is exciting, challenging, and rewarding. Adventure shows kids that faith is not boring.

THEY EXPERIENCE COMMUNITY. Trips provide the opportunity for kids to love, to build up, and to support each other. They get a brief taste of what togetherness and unity can be like.

THEY EXPERIENCE SPIRITUAL THINGS. Trips give kids the freedom to let go of their worldly concerns and focus on spiritual issues.

THEY EXPERIENCE NEW THINGS. It is a thrill to do something that you have never done before. Trips allow kids to experience this in a variety of ways. For some, it's their first time away from home. For others, it might be their first time to ski, to ride a horse, or to shoot a BB gun. Trips help kids discover skills that can last a lifetime.

THEY EXPERIENCE SIGNIFICANCE. Trips let kids discover, through both success and failure, that they are important and significant. They can be stars in a world where they are often considered average.

THEY EXPERIENCE CHRISTIANITY AT WORK. I have always felt it is important for junior highers to see that Christianity exists *and* that it works outside their own worlds. Going someplace helps them to see this in action. God works in other places beside their own church and youth group.

TYPES OF CAMPS, TRIPS, AND RETREATS

When you are considering the type of camp experience to provide for your kids, you must first think through needs. My home church used to put it this way: "Find a need and fill it, find a hurt and heal it." It's a smart philosophy. Once you have determined the needs of your kids, it is time to decide the medium that you will use to meet those needs. This is where our creativity gets to kick in, oh boy! Let's check out some of our options.

RESIDENT CAMPS. This camp is where your kids reside at a permanent site; you have two ways of going here. One, you can go to a place where the camp runs the program. This is great if you want to concentrate on being with your kids without the pressure of running program details. Many camps and conference centers (especially the larger ones) do this. Some denominations will host them as well. Two, you can rent out a resident camp and run your own program. Although this requires a lot more work, it allows you to design the program to meet your specific needs. In my program, I do both. For our winter retreat, we go to a nearby Christian conference center where everything is pretty much taken care of. Our other main camps (fall, spring, and summer) are ones that I create around the needs of our kids.

A great way to run your own program at camp is to pull another church in and run the camp with them. I do this quite a bit. There are many advantages: You get to do an event with a youth minister friend, your kids meet Christian kids from another church, you are able to combine your program resources, and the increased attendance from the combined groups enables you to meet minimums that some camps require for exclusive use of their facilities.

TRAVEL CAMPS. On travel camps, the group travels from site to site. Groups can travel by car, van, bus, motor home, train, plane, or boat. Besides being loads of fun (and lots of work), there is nothing like traveling with a group of kids. People think I'm crazy, but I really mean it. It seems like I am able to accomplish more in a week-long travel camp than I can in a season full of meetings.

Last summer I took a group of kids on a travel camp we called "The Wild West Travel Trek." For ten days we traveled around California in search of adventure. We went river rafting, jet skied around a beautiful lake, rode cable cars in San Francisco, and explored a variety of forests and towns. Actually some of the best parts of the trip were the spontaneous things that happened. While we structured time for input and had the kids keep daily journals, we allowed for enough freedom in the schedule to "flow." Got a limited budget? Try staying in churches along the way (be sure to contact them well ahead of time and take extra care to leave their places spick-and-span).

CAMPING TRIPS. Instead of staying in a facility, try camping outside. It's pretty inexpensive and, depending on where you live, it gives you many options of places to go. Lists of camping areas can be found by checking out the travel section at your local bookstore (try your library, too). You can also get good information from the auto club and by writing the national and state parks departments. The only drawback to camping is the need for equipment. You can usually get around this by borrowing from kids and parents. Another option is renting equipment from a sporting goods, camping, or mountaineering store. If you have the budget, you might consider investing in a few camping supplies for your church. I have done this with my church, and the equipment has more than paid for itself in its use.

SPECIALTY TRIPS. These trips include snow skiing, waterskiing, fishing, rock climbing, surfing, tractor pulling, and the like. This is a great way to bring in kids who wouldn't normally come to a church event. Each winter our group sponsors a weekend ski trip to the Sierra Nevada Mountains. Everybody, churched and unchurched alike, loves going on the trip. We encourage our kids to bring their friends—it's a wonderful outreach opportunity. Specialty trips are also good for teaching. Rock climbing is a great example. If you want to teach "trust" to kids, rock climbing does the trick (I am currently planning a father/son rock climbing trip to teach this very fact). Special note: This is a great way of getting adults to become active in your program. You can recruit help from people who are experts in specialty areas—a fisherman, a great skier, and so on. You can use their instruction *and* their equipment!

RECREATION RETREATS. Getting away "just to play" has validity. Don't feel embarrassed about it. If the needs of your group would be met by this type of retreat, then go for it. Recreation can be celebration, not just goofing off. One encouragement, however—be sure to look for "teachable moments" while you are playing. These moments are opportunities that occur in life situations that can become launching pads for discussion. With this in mind, even a trip to an amusement park is loaded with spiritual possibilities.

CORE/OUTREACH RETREATS. You can do a special retreat with your Christian core kids or an outreach retreat to draw in unchurched kids. Both are important. A retreat with your core kids enables you to concentrate on deeper issues. Not only is it important, it is very refreshing. When you spend so much time in ministry just trying to convince kids to follow Christ, it's wonderful to spend time with

a group that really desires to grow.

An outreach camp is important, too. I know many adults who credit a youth camp as the place where they first met Christ—remember that.

We should also remember to be responsible with our powers of persuasion. Junior highers can often be very emotional and can be easily pushed toward almost anything. As ministers, we must be very careful in these moments. While I understand and have experienced the power of God moving through a group of kids, I also understand that manipulating kids toward decisions is not smart.

It is essential to be very up-front with parents about what the trip is all about. Many unchurched families are very apprehensive about church camps. They have fears that we brainwash their kids. To ease their minds (and to show them integrity), mail a pretrip letter to parents. The letter should include what to bring, where you are going, what you are doing, who the staff members are, when you are leaving and returning, where you can be contacted, and other pertinent information. Also, send parents of new kids a brief biography on yourself. This is a very valuable (and appreciated) practice. Don't get me wrong—our goal is that kids meet and experience Christ in everything we do, but we need to be responsible. Trust is essential for a youth worker. It takes a long time to gain it and a second to lose it.

LEADERSHIP RETREATS. If you have student leaders in your ministry, many good things can be accomplished by taking them away for a retreat. You can plan out the year's schedule, coordinate an upcoming major event, reward them at the end of a term of service, pray for the ministry, or teach discipleship.

SPECIAL RELATIONSHIP TRIPS. Great experiences result when you design trips around special relationships (father and son, mother and daughter, father and daughter, or mother and son; how about father and pet, mom and cousin?). Try doing special trips just for boys or just for girls. This is especially helpful in dealing with such issues as sex, dating, and relationships. Encourage your staff leaders to do little mini-retreats (overnights and sleepovers) with kids of the same sex. Wonderful things result in talks over popcorn or around the basketball hoop.

MISSIONS TRIPS. Don't panic. Although trips to faraway lands are certainly part of the picture, missions also include your local world. Projects close to home help keep costs low and organization struggles at a minimum (hopefully). For some great ideas on where to go or what to do, be sure to look closely at Darrell's valuable insight in Chapter Eleven.

CREATIVITY IN CAMPING

Do you like to look at stars? I can literally spend hours gazing into the infinite vastness of a clear night sky. Unfortunately, I don't get to do this very often. In the Los Angeles area, the glare from the city lights prevents you from seeing much. When you get outside the city, however, and stand in the desert or the mountains, the brilliance is awesome. Creativity is similar to this experience. There is so much potential for brilliance out there, but it is often hidden. The glare from tradition, lack of funds, inexperience, or lack of support keeps us from finding the creative options that are available to us. They are there, but sometimes we just can't see them.

Having trouble seeing through the glare? Don't worry, the potential for creative camps, trips, and retreats is out there. Here are a few ways to catch sight of them.

ASSOCIATE WITH CREATIVE PEOPLE. I mentioned earlier that a wonderful way of tapping into creativity is to do trips with other youth workers and their groups. Each summer I coordinate a week-long camp with nine other churches from our area. During the months before the camp, I gather the youth leaders from the churches for a series of planning meetings. I am astounded at the amount of creativity that flows through those meetings. We are able to play off each others' ideas and come up with some pretty hot programs. Hey, there is nothing spectacular about us, but when we're put together, some pretty brilliant things come out. Try calling a youth ministry buddy and asking him or her to join your next retreat. You might also call or meet with a couple of sharp youth workers from your area and pick their brains on their best camp ideas.

HAVE HEALTHY DISSATISFACTION. Some of the most creative people I know are those who are dissatisfied with the way it's always been done. After a retreat, they are always looking for ways to make the trip better. Because most camps are pretty hard work, we are often satisfied just to get it over with. Don't settle for that. Pour your creative energy into it—you'll probably enjoy it more!

A sense of healthy dissatisfaction will also keep your trips fresh. Kids love it when old programs are given new twists. This is why evaluation is so important after your trip. If I fail to evaluate immediately after a trip, I usually forget the things that needed changing and end up repeating my mistakes. Write out your thoughts, both good and bad, and keep them in a file. These notes will be valuable once the following year rolls around.

VARY YOUR APPROACH. Creativity means options—don't be afraid to use them. Consider trying different methods (even if the ones you use are working) just to keep kids guessing. It is wiser to keep a step ahead of your kids by switching your style *before* they tire of it. Special note: Creativity and tradition don't have to be at odds with each other. A sense of tradition, especially with camps, is important and valuable. This might be found by using the same facility every year, by doing annual trips, or by repeating special experiences each year. Camps allow us to create memories that kids will use as guideposts for the rest of their lives. Vary your approach, but keep some tradition.

OBSERVE AND COLLECT. I have heard a number of people describe the art of creativity as "the ability to copy." Although I don't like that definition and don't necessarily agree with it, I understand its concept. Nothing is really ever created, it is simply redesigned. In light of this, start collecting ideas from successful groups, camps, trips, and retreats. Try getting on the mailing list of some junior high church ministries and Christian camps around the country. You might also keep a collection of brochures for graphic and printing ideas. Perhaps you might set aside a weekend to travel around to different area camps or retreat centers, check out their facilities, and pick the brains of their program people. When you return home, set up a file of your camping options for future use.

ASK SMART QUESTIONS. Creativity is often simply applying common sense. If you are wise enough to ask yourself the right questions, everyone will attribute your success to creativity. Here are a few questions to get you started.

A FEW SMART QUESTIONS TO ASK

1. What would I like to do?
2. What would the kids like to do?
3. What are the needs of the kids?
4. What can we afford?
5. Where can we go?
6. How far is it?
7. How long will it take to get there?
8. How good or how poor is the facility?
9. How much will it cost?
10. Who can go?
11. Who can be counseling staff?
12. Who can be programming staff?
13. What equipment do we need?
14. What could go wrong?
15. What could go right?

GO WITH THE FLOW. As in any event involving junior highers, be ready to be flexible. Don't panic when the programs that you worked on for months become "undoable" because of some circumstance. One of the best weekend retreats I recall is the one when it rained during the entire trip. Everything I had planned went down the tube. After some quick reworking, we ended up incorporating the rain into the program. We played mud games, built mini-boats and raced them, created a slip and slide on the lawn, and more. It was a blast. It's smart to have options already designed, but when you can't . . . relax. Look at it as your big opportunity to impress everyone with your creativity. It is amazing what you can come up with when you are backed into a corner!

CAMP DETAILS

I remember the first camp I ever created on my own. Although good things came out of it, I was lucky it wasn't a complete disaster. I don't think I realized it, but I had no idea what it took to pull off the retreat. It was definitely a "Steve Dickie Wingarama." Experience has taught me the importance of thinking through details prior to the trip. Here are a few to add to your checklist.

THEMES. My retreats usually focus around a spiritual theme. Determined by the needs of the group, the spiritual theme is the one "big idea" that I want the group to own. This theme packages teaching and input times. Throw in a fun theme. This gives the camp the crazy, off-the-wall flow that's important to junior high ministry, and it's also great in promoting and marketing the camp. You can build fun themes around just about any topic. The following are some all-time favorites:

1. "Missing Teddies"—The first night of camp, kidnap all the stuffed animals that the kids brought on the retreat. Run a theme around the mystery of who stole them and how to get them back.
2. "Raiders of the Lost Aardvark"—Do an entire parody of the famous Indiana Jones flicks.
3. "The Adventures of Conan"—Have Conan the Barbarian become various characters (Conan the Librarian, Conan the Seminarian, and so on).

I once even built a crazy theme around the idea that the Cartwrights from *Bonanza* go back in time to help Robin Hood find his self-esteem. In building a fun theme, it's fun to carry an idea or a skit throughout the event in a serial fashion or through a series of episodes.

SCHEDULE. Once the theme of the retreat is determined, it's important to organize those thoughts into a schedule. Even though this seems obvious, many youth workers fail to detail their planning. Opportunities can slip by when we fail to schedule. When planning a retreat, take a piece of paper, turn it lengthwise, and draw five columns. In the far left column, list a need of your group. Moving to the right, list a goal to meet that need, then list a program activity to meet the goal. Next, detail the equipment needed for the activity. In the far column, assign a leader to organize the activity. Not only does this ensure your schedule needs, it also helps your staff know why you're doing the activity. Keep your staff on top of the schedule, but keep the details a mystery to the kids. Keep them guessing by constantly throwing surprises at them; you don't want kids deciding what they won't like before it happens. A word of advice: Be willing to be flexible with your schedule. Your best laid plans will often be changed. Schedule options for yourself.

PROMOTION. You can have the hottest camp around, but if it isn't properly promoted, then it could flop (believe me, I know). Here are a few hot ideas.

CREATIVE PROMOTION IDEAS

1. Visit the site and shoot a fun video (or slides).
2. Create posters and signs and plaster them throughout your meeting rooms and facility.
3. Create a great brochure or flyer and mail it to students.
4. Write announcements for your

church newsletter and Sunday bulletin.

5. Invite resident camp staff members to come to your church to make an announcement, show slides or a video, or answer questions.
6. Set up a table, manned by your staff or the kids, with camp promotional material.
7. Create a time line with due dates for promotional efforts.
8. Hit the phones—call the kids and their parents.
9. Offer a discount for those who register early.
10. Offer a prize to the person who brings the most friends.
11. Offer a free dinner to the staff leader who gets the most kids to register for camp.
12. Make verbal announcements from your church pulpit.
13. Do a crazy skit with your staff and kids at your group meeting.
14. Give camp T-shirts to kids who register early. They serve as good ads for kids who have yet to sign up.
15. Hold a summer camp information meeting for parents.
16. Have kids who have gone to camp before tell about their experiences.
17. Give your camp a great catchy title.
18. Invite the speaker or the music group to come to your church for a speaking session or concert.
19. Do tongue-in-cheek interviews on video (garbage man talking about camp food).
20. Offer to include items in the camp price (a set of tapes of the speaker's talk, a T-shirt, a book about the topic being discussed, a 1965 Corvette, $50,000 in video arcade tokens, a train trip to Hawaii).

COUNSELORS AND STAFF. Running a trip, a camp, or a retreat is hard work, so get all the help you can . . . plus some. Define your program areas and delegate responsibility to key people. Depending on the size of your group and the availability of qualified leaders, you might delegate responsibility for spiritual input, recreation, music, discipline, counselor encouragement, food service, water sports, sound and lighting, and the like. Also, make sure you have a good core of counselors who are mature enough to carry this important responsibility. Apart from the kids, these folks are the most important people at camp. Besides being in the best position to minister directly to the kids, they sleep, eat, talk, discuss, play, work, laugh, and cry with them. A camp speaker can challenge kids, but the counselor is the one who can really drive home the application. Depending on the event, try for one counselor to every five to eight kids. Below are a few qualifications taken from the counselor training program at Northern California's Mount Hermon Christian Conference Center.[2] Much of what I have learned about ministry has been gleaned from my years on staff there and from the mentoring of Dick Dosker, their retired director of junior high camping.

COUNSELING PRINCIPLES MOUNT HERMON CHRISTIAN CONFERENCE CENTER— REDWOOD CAMP

1. **BE RESPECTED**—Always make your aim ultimate respect versus immediate popularity.
2. **BE EXPECTANT**—Always expect the best from your campers.
3. **BE ACCEPTING OF DIFFER-**

ENCES—Always avoid categorizing people.

4. **BE A TEACHER**—Always seek to stretch children—balance the physical, mental, social, and spiritual.

5. **BE ENTHUSIASTIC**—Always be supportive of program activities.

6. **BE PATIENT**—Always realize that trusting relationships take time to develop.

7. **BE A MODEL**—Always remember that you're being watched.

8. **BE AN IN-PROCESS PERSON**—Always help campers know that you're still growing, maturing, and discovering with them.

9. **BE A LISTENER**—Always listen for true feelings rather than surface words.

10. **BE UNDERSTANDING**—Always try to "feel with" the campers, helping them feel understood and worthy.

11. **BE AFFIRMING**—Always try to offer positive reinforcement. Compliment positive behavior.

12. **BE HONEST**—Always be willing to admit that you're wrong.

13. **BE SHOCKPROOF**—Always avoid a shocked reaction to personal horror stories.

14. **BE CONFIDENT**—Always keep the trust of those who share in confidence.

15. **BE FAIR**—Always make the punishment fit the misbehavior.

16. **BE ACCOUNTABLE**—Always know where your campers are. When apart, let them know where you'll be and when you'll meet them next.

17. **BE IN CONTROL**—Always let children know your boundaries and expectations.

18. **BE WILLING TO CONFRONT**—Always help a camper see the need to decide, act on that decision, and assume responsibility for that choice.

19. **BE WILLING TO ACCEPT LONG-RANGE RESULTS**—Always remember that God has called us simply to be faithful. Avoid high pressure.

20. **BE WILLING TO LET THE HOLY SPIRIT WORK**—Always prayerfully depend on the Spirit's timing in all matters.

BUDGET AND FINANCES. When planning a camp, create three budgets—worst case, probable, and best case. This will help you anticipate any losses and use any gains. Figure the fixed costs first: camp facility rental, food, and transportation. Then start adding program expenses, both necessities and your dream list: recreation supplies, special events, honorarium, publicity, snacks, and so on. Once the overall cost of the trip is determined, divide it by the number of kids you anticipate will attend to arrive at the fee to be charged. If the fee is too high, go back to your program expenses and start trimming from the wish list until the fee is reasonable. If you are planning a trip you've never done before, plan for a worst case scenario (low attendance), and be sure to keep records for next year. It would be valuable to sit down with experienced youth workers from your area and glean from their experiences if this is all new to you.

RULES AND EXPECTATIONS. I am convinced that junior highers desire rules because they give kids a sense of security in the midst of a changing environment. Kids, however, will certainly crash up against those boundaries, if just to test them, so be prepared for any possibility. In the book *The Complete Book of Youth*

Ministry, Michael Risley believes that a good rule for discipline during summer camps is based on the "three P's":[3] privacy (no boys in the girls' cabins and vice versa); property (take care of it; if you break it, you buy it!); and program (all meals, meetings, and activities are mandatory). Try being creative in how you present your rules. My favorite is to have a group of staff leaders do an impersonation of a typical group of junior highers. You can have a lot of fun, the kids laugh, and you communicate the rules in a positive way.

HEALTH AND SAFETY. There is never room for messing around here, my friends. The youth worker's greatest nightmare is for a mishap to occur under his or her leadership. Although problems can't always be avoided, stupidity can; prevention is the key. Spend some time going through your camp schedule looking for all possible disasters, think through emergency plans to deal with each problem, and have a written emergency plan available for your staff. Here are a few other important things to do.

1. *Always* carry medical release forms. Rather than collecting one for every event, have parents complete one that is good for the entire year. *Don't leave home without it!*
2. Designate a parent to be a contact person in charge of a list of campers and their parents' phone numbers. In an emergency (or if you are delayed in your return), the contact parent can call the other parents.
3. Keep an emergency first aid kit with you at all times. You might even send yourself and your staff through a first aid course.
4. Keep a credit card and cash with you

for the unexpected.
5. Get an emergency road service card; mine has gotten me out of countless jams.
6. Obtain information about hospitals and clinics close to where you are traveling.
7. Have a group of people committed to praying for your group as you travel.

FOOD. When you travel to a resident camp, the food is often included with the fee. The camp staff prepares the food and your kids simply eat and, er . . . uh . . . enjoy it. When you coordinate other types of camping experiences, you may cook your own food. With smart shopping, you can make pretty good meals affordably (my interns from past years will laugh at me about that one—I'm infamous for bargain food shopping). Assign food purchasing and cooking to your leaders and use kids for preparation and cleanup. It's also a good idea to bring a core group of high school kids to a junior high camp and let them be in charge of all food services. They can run their own leadership meetings on the side. Don't want to cook? Our kids would just as soon eat pizza from a local restaurant. You can sometimes swing pretty good deals from restaurants when you have a large group.

TRANSPORTATION. I always tell our staff members that camp begins in the church parking lot. The ride to our trip site is half the fun. Prepare a travel pack for the ride, which includes a letter about the trip, a map of how to get there, some jokes and stories, trivia questions, paper games (tic-tac-toe, hangman), and numerous odds and ends. These help keep a long trip "rideable." If your church doesn't own vehicles (don't feel bad, they always break down anyway), you can rent a bus (driver included) or rent vans and drive them yourself. Be sure to check with your state's motor vehicle department regarding van license laws. Liability is nothing to mess around with. You might try asking staff leaders or parents to drive (become friendly with parents with vans!).

AFTER THE CAMP

Be sure to take advantage of the wonderful follow-up opportunities after the camp experience. I must admit that I have often gone to incredible measures to create a great camp, only to lose much of the spiritual results because I didn't follow up with kids. Write the campers notes to challenge them to continue to grow in all that they've learned. You might also create a special group to meet for a period of weeks after the camp. Following last year's summer camp, we gave all our kids a Bible signed by each of the staff members (the Bible became a way for the kids to remember their camp commitments). A final idea is to hold a reunion a few months following the camp. Bring back the camp speaker, show slides and video shot at camp, and rekindle the flame that was lit at camp.

It's also important for the leader to spend time praying for the kids and thanking God for his faithfulness. Write out the victories and rewards that surfaced from the trip experience. When it's time to start planning your next retreat, pull out the list to remind yourself that despite the headaches—the van breaking down, counselors cancelling at the last minute, your failure to bring your talk notes, the wildest kids in your group acting like it, and it raining the entire trip—the end result is all worth it. And you know what? It is!

ENDNOTES

1. Anthony Campolo, *Growing Up in America: A Sociology of Youth Ministry* (Grand Rapids: YS/Zondervan, 1989), 125.
2. Mount Hermon Christian Conference Center, Mount Hermon, CA 95041.
3. Michael Risley, "Strategies for Summer Camp as Part of the Church Ministry," in Warren S. Benson and Mark Senter, III, eds., *The Complete Book of Youth Ministry* (Chicago: Moody Press, 1987), 380.

CHAPTER NINE

CREATIVE IDEAS FOR SMALL GROUP MINISTRY

By Darrell Pearson

No matter what the actual size of your group, whether it's eight kids or eighty, you need to be effective working with a small group of students. Why? Because it is crucial for a group of people to know one another and to share their thoughts and feelings, especially if it's a group of junior highers. People need to be in a small group setting so that others know what is going on in their lives.

WHAT A SMALL GROUP IS

Several years ago, in an eighth grade Sunday school class, I asked the question, "Has anybody had to make an important decision this week?" I waited for a few seconds while the kids pondered my question. When no one responded, I asked several of the girls the question directly. One mumbled something about cleaning up her room, the other about what she was going to wear to school. All of a sudden a quiet boy in the corner spoke: "I had to decide whether to live with my mom or my dad." All heads jerked around to look at him, amazed at his response, and all were instantly empathetic with the tough decision he faced. What if he had not been in a small group where he could share this? What if he had kept his thoughts to himself? By his willingness to talk, he opened himself up to others' help. It wasn't long before someone else asked him how he made the decision, and soon he was sharing many things about his life. Small groups are important!

The problem, of course, is that small groups can seem incredibly boring or intimidating. My goal in this chapter is to share some thoughts that might add spice to your small group experiences.

WHAT A SMALL GROUP IS NOT

Remember that small groups are a time for growing—not a time for ragging on others. It's easy to let a small and intimate group become a gossip session, so be careful that your group remains focused on the goal at hand. I recently allowed a group of students to start laughing and joking about a new member in the group (it seemed like it was just in fun), but it soon got out of hand. One person left in tears because, unknown to everyone else, she had quietly fostered a new friendship with him. I learned my lesson the hard way.

THE BEST AND THE . . .

Take a few moments to remember the worst small group experience you have been a part of. Maybe it was a class you took, a Bible study you were in, an office training program—just about anything except a junior high group you've led! Briefly analyze why is was so awful.

THE SETTING. Describe the physical arrangements: the way you sat, the room you were in, the lighting, and so on. Was there anything about the setting that was completely negative? Was it held at a particularly bad time?

THE LEADER. Often a small group experience is bad because the leadership is bad. Describe the good and the bad points of the leader. Was he or she prepared and knowledgeable? Did you feel good being in the leader's presence?

THE TOPIC. Was this something you were interested in or were you forced to attend? Were your expectations too high? Explain the topic or material and describe what was good and what was bad about it.

THE PARTICIPANTS. Who was in this group? Did they know each other? Was there time for discussion?

Imagine a junior higher trying to survive this situation. Even *you* couldn't handle it. Study your responses and think about your last small group encounter with your students. Did you repeat any of the negatives?

Now, consider a great small group experience you had, and analyze it in the same way: the setting, the leader, the topic, and the participants. What made this one work? What can you learn from the positive small group meeting that you can use with junior highers?

A colleague of mine has a small group of eighth grade boys who meet for Bible study every week. I was amazed that James could get this kind of commitment out of them. I asked him how long they met each time. "Two hours," he responded. Two hours! That can seem like an eternity with eighth graders—it *is* an eternity with eighth graders! "How do you study the Bible for two hours?" I asked. "Easy. We wrestle for the first hour, study for forty-five minutes, then eat before we close." James had discovered a great secret for effective junior high small groups: provide an appropriate and comfortable environment!

MOTIVATING STUDENTS TO JOIN

Getting junior highers to commit to a small group might seem like an impossibility, but with the right approach, it will be received in a positive manner. Some students will respond to a creative mailing that outlines a new small group for kids interested in leadership development; others will respond to a personal, one-on-one invitation encouraging their involvement; still others will respond through parental suggestions that you have cultivated in parent meetings. If you expect a lot from students, you'll get it. Why not expect a response to a small group activity? There are always students willing to try something new and stretching. (Of course, don't forget the main motivator that will get kids to come: serve doughnuts!)

The first Bible study I started years ago, called "Meateaters," met with major apathy when I mentioned it to my whole junior high group. But when I sent out notes outlining the details, including that it was only for students willing to chew on the faith a bit deeper, I had a dozen students return their cards and commit to join the group. It wasn't easy in the beginning. It took the motivator of an overnight lock-in to make it seem fun, but it took hold and ministered to some extra-sharp students. Of course, I still had to buy doughnuts.

LEADERSHIP STYLE

How you lead your kids, and how they perceive they are led, is vitally important for small group success. Authoritarian style by itself doesn't usually work well with junior highers ("I thought I told you to shut up!"). Democratic style often goes nowhere ("Anybody else think we should do something different?"). Laissez-faire results in nobody caring to attend ("What do you guys think we should do tonight?"). It's best to encompass many different styles of leadership, using parts of all three. Of course, you have to lead in the way you feel most comfortable. Sometimes it's good to be direct and authoritarian; other times it's best to scrap the plan and go with the flow; and it's even appropriate sometimes to let the students determine

the direction. At the center of good leadership, however, is always a person who keeps the group moving forward toward the goal that has been set.

Roberta Hestenes, president of Eastern College and a well-known expert in the field of small groups, has suggested that there are "seven C's" to keeping a small group effective.[1]

1. Covenant (a shared understanding of the group's purpose).
2. Commitment (the disciplines the group has agreed on to accomplish its goals).
3. Caring (members learning to love each other).
4. Content (centering on Scripture).
5. Communication (the glue binding members together in love).
6. Crying/conflict/congruence (feelings cannot be denied and are an important part of life).
7. Christ (the center who transforms life).

No matter what your leadership style, you can help a group grow by keeping the "seven C's" in mind.

DISCUSSION TECHNIQUES

How do you get kids to open up and talk in a small group? Every junior high worker has experienced that dreadful moment when no one will answer the simplest of questions, and you start wondering how you will fill the next thirty-five minutes.

First, don't be scared by silence. We all have a tendency to feel uncomfortable every time there is a break in the action. When you ask a question of a group of kids, give them time to think through a response. They might not be inattentive, just processing. Avoid filling the gap with inane words.

Second, do your best not to be judgmental about any comment that you disagree with. Be supportive—find something positive in the response, or let the group's comments guide the person back. Don't jump on the person answering, or no one will be courageous enough to test the waters on the next question. Say something like, "Good. Can anyone add to that?" or "I suppose that's one way to see it. Are there other thoughts?" It's so easy to react to a testy junior higher's response with criticism and unnecessary advice. Do your best to support the kids' efforts, no matter how feeble they might seem to you.

Third, feel free to suggest something controversial or stimulating that might get kids to react. You can always disclaim yourself later. It doesn't hurt to get them thinking by challenging a common value, such as questioning a popular music or sports hero.

During our divorce recovery workshop discussions, it's often a difficult moment when kids who have just met sit in a circle and attempt to talk. A pointed statement challenging common ground perceptions always gets a response. Instead of centering on divorce, sometimes we have to start with rap or hairstyles or sports. It gets things started.

Finally, don't let one person dominate the discussion. Feel free to direct the kids' behavior so that you are in control. Sit forward in your chair, even if they don't. Use your hands to slow someone down by pointing or holding out a hand as if you're about to put it on the kid's shoulder—but don't actually touch them. Eye contact is crucial. The kids know you're in control, so whomever you look

at gets the floor. If you keep looking at the person talking, he or she will keep talking. If you look at others, you'll encourage someone else's participation.

GAMES

Junior highers need to play. Even in the context of small groups that are designed to be serious, kids need the fun and challenge of a game to stimulate them to action. Have you played the game where the members of a group of five to twenty reach into the center of a circle, grab two different people's hands with each of theirs, then try and untangle the mess without letting go of the hands they've grabbed? It's a great game that works every time. If you haven't played it, the kids end up in a big circle with their hands joined together.

Simple name games work well. Try the one where each member breaks off a piece of thread (any length). Once all the kids have a piece, tell them to wind it around one finger. Every time they make a loop, they have to tell the group something about themselves. The people who broke off the longest pieces tell the most. Another favorite is "Two Truths and a Lie." The kids tell three things about themselves—two true and one false—and the group has to guess which one is the lie.

SIMULATION GAMES

On a more serious level, simulation games can be a great tool for small groups. A simulation game attempts to recreate a real situation through a role-played experience. The game is designed to teach students something about the original reality. For example, having your small group simulate that it is the governing board of your church can make for an interesting discussion tool. Each member might be given a specific role or personality to play, and he or she has to make decisions about an issue facing the church. The ensuing discussion will raise the students' awareness of real-life situations or problems. You'll be amazed at their creativity.

My favorite simulation game is centered on the unfair economic balance in the world. Divide your kids into several small groups with each group assigned the name of a specific country. Each group has a ten-minute "day" of work to complete a task: For example, Panama workers might fill cups of water, walk across the room, and deposit the water into a bucket. A student chosen to oversee the Panama group is given a specific amount of money to pay out in salaries at the end of the day. A second country has a different task that is even more repetitious and boring. Its work leader has less money to pay out in salaries. At the close of the first "day" of work, the workers are paid. However, for the next day of work, the work leaders are told that they can hire all but one person in the group, or they have to pay less salary to everybody (keeping more for themselves of course), or there is a natural disaster and less work all around. The goal is to earn the most money. Kids will get frustrated as they struggle to get hired each day, and work leaders will be frustrated that they can't help everyone equally. You are the overall boss—if a work leader is not getting the job done, hire another kid and make the former work leader a laborer.

After a few periods of playing, you will find that some kids have done well, some are angry, and some have figured out how

to be creative. I've had kids request to marry someone else in the game to be able to share their money, and I've had kids go on strike for better working conditions. Simulation games take lots of interesting turns that you can never predict. What you can predict is that junior highers will learn something significant—if you've planned the game correctly.

At the end of play, have an auction to sell candy bars. The kids in poorer countries will be furious that they have less money, even though they played as hard. Tough lesson, but one best learned through a simulation game.

For a detailed listing of a game similar to the one I have just described, write Compassion International (P.O. Box 7000, Colorado Springs, CO 80933) and get their Compassion Project. It contains a great simulation game that is easy to play.

There are three keys for playing great simulation games: having good concepts and goals for the games (what do you wish to teach?); having simple formats that can be learned quickly; and having enough space to allow the kids some freedom to create on their own.

TYPES OF SMALL GROUPS

BIBLE STUDY. Yes, it's possible to get junior highers to study the Bible together. On a basic level, they want to know how to live and how to get along with others. Any junior high Bible study ought to keep a strong focus on relationships and what the Bible says about them. Be practical. Although it's important to teach Bible history, word usage, and the context of each passage (what is the Bible accurately saying?), junior high kids need a great deal of down-to-earth study (what does it mean for me today?). Aim for inductive study, in which the kids discover for themselves what's in the book, rather than being told what it says.

A creative touch is also important. Use object lessons from the passage so that the kids can feel and touch something tangible that teaches truth. The Bible's discussions of figs, olives, wheat, and other items from daily life lend themselves to great Bible study ideas (fig newtons . . . green olives . . . wheat germ). Every page of Scripture has something you can use as a jumping off point.

Incidentally, I don't care much for the Bible study guides in which kids fill in the blank lines. It doesn't seem creative to me. Take the time to work at it—it will pay off in interested students!

SHARING GROUPS. We recently started a small sharing group called "Grow in the Dark." The concept is simple: Whoever shows up hops in the van, travels to some unknown and often bizarre location, and then sits in a circle while we sing, share, and pray. I've been amazed at the response—there are a lot of hurting kids who love to get together and share problems. If it seems improbable that kids in your group would get into this, think back—have you ever asked them to participate in sharing? Expect a lot, get a lot.

In the midst of a crisis (parents' divorce, a relative's death, an acquaintance's suicide attempt), friends are often open to forming a sharing group to struggle through the issue. Their crisis is a ministry opportunity for you—and them.

PROJECT GROUPS. Junior high students (especially the younger ones) still enjoy working on skills and projects, though they won't always admit it. A small group can focus on a number of projects. At our last two summer camps,

more kids signed up for a class on silk screening T-shirts than any other class (they had a choice of fifteen classes). Why not take an interest level like this and form a small group to learn a specific skill.

LEADERSHIP GROUPS. Junior highers are interested in becoming somebody. They love leadership development that helps them learn the skills they need to minister to others, especially younger students. A great small group can focus on those interested in learning what it takes to make things happen in the world.

SERVICE GROUPS. A small, committed core of students makes an excellent service group, designed to carry out some specific ministry on an ongoing basis. I recently heard of a group of junior high boys who committed themselves to maintain a small plot of land by a sculpture in a park. It doesn't take a lot of work; just enough to let them get together and accomplish something. The fellowship of working together provides the context for some solid growing.

Small groups—they can be frustrating sometimes, particularly with junior high students. But if you move past the boundaries we normally set for kids and expect a lot from them, they'll surprise you with their commitment and enthusiasm. If you keep on the creative side of the program, you'll set the pattern for students to grow. Small groups are the best way to touch the needs of kids—they need to be known by someone else!

ENDNOTES

1. Roberta Hestenes, *Christian Formation and Discipleship* (Pasadena, Calif.: Fuller Theological Seminary, 1984), 23.

CHAPTER TEN

CREATIVE DISCIPLE MAKING

By Steve Dickie

An older ministry friend once offered me this piece of advice when I first started working with junior high kids: More is caught than taught.

Smart friend. She knew that if I was looking for quick results and immediate rewards in my teaching, I could become one frustrated youth worker. If I was going to change the lives of kids, my up-front ability was only going to get me so far. It would be the hours I spent outside the classroom that would end up making the difference. More kids would probably catch the message of Christ over an ice cream cone after school or around a basketball hoop on a Saturday morning than in one of my brilliant talks. The years have proven my friend's advice to be sound.

I first began to realize the validity of this concept when I saw my junior highers imitating me. They began to use some of my slang expressions, follow my favorite sport teams and music groups, and even buy clothes like mine. Look, I'm not exactly "Joe Trendsetter," but I guess I'm cool enough that some kids actually wanted to imitate me. I quickly learned (with sobering responsibility) that this gave me the power to influence them through the way I lived. They were watching me, and I had the wonderful opportunity to teach God's great truth by modeling it to them.

THE STYLE OF THE MASTER

Teaching through modeling was the way Jesus himself did ministry. Instead of simply gathering large crowds and amassing converts, he chose to gather twelve men and focus much of his three years of public ministry on them. They became *disciples*, which comes from the New Testament word *mathetes*, meaning a taught or trained one. Ron Lee Davis describes this process in his book, *Mentoring: The Strategy of the Master.*

> When Jesus taught the twelve about servanthood, not only did he teach them verbally, but he washed their feet. When he taught the twelve about prayer, not only did he teach them what to pray, he took them into the garden and prayed with them. Whatever Jesus wanted to teach the twelve, he taught them not only with words, but by *immersing* them in the experience of his life.[1]

Jesus knew what he was doing. He knew that once he left the earth, the good news of God's love for the world would be carried on by the disciples. From generation to generation, faithful men and women would pass the message on to others. Who would have figured it? Through the ministry of making disciples, Jesus literally turned the world upside down. I encourage you to pick up a copy of Robert Coleman's *The Master Plan of Evangelism.*[2] This classic helps us see how Jesus used disciple making to carry his message into the world.

A WISE INVESTMENT

After his death and resurrection, Jesus gathered his followers and told them to "go make disciples of all nations." His earthly ministry was done. He had planted the seed in his disciples and it was now their turn to carry the message into the world. It would start small, but soon spread like wildfire.

Jesus' strategy has always amazed me. You'd figure he would enter the world with a lot of flash. As a kid I thought he would have been smarter to have made himself eighty feet tall, changed his voice to a loudspeaker, and cruised through the world making his point. That would certainly grab people's attention. If he came back today, we'd probably have him hooked up with a Madison Avenue advertising firm. We'd book him on talk shows and have his picture plastered on billboards everywhere. We might even schedule an international tour with contemporary Christian music's top recording group opening for him. Obviously, he had something else in mind. By focusing on the few, he had an impact on many . . . or as Ron Lee Davis describes, "More time with fewer people equals greater lasting impact for God."[3] Disciple making is a wise investment.

IT MAKES SENSE

Jesus' Great Commission to make disciples makes sense for junior high ministry. Here are a few reasons why.

IT GIVES US HOPE. Earlier in the book, I shared that one of the greatest frustrations for junior high workers is the lack of immediate results. We pour our energies into kids and often don't get to see our efforts come into fruition. Disciple making becomes our hope. When we realize that our efforts are going to be rewarded in the long run, it helps us stick with it. Investing our lives in kids' lives is going to reap long-term results.

THE MATHEMATICS ARE SOUND. In his book *The Making of a Disciple*, Dr. Keith Phillips shares the power of the geometric progression in discipleship.

> Suppose on the first day I led one person to Christ. Subsequently, I led another individual to Christ every

day for the rest of the year. By the end of the year I would have directed 365 people to the Lord. If I continued to do that for the next thirty-two years, I would have reached 11,680. Quite an accomplishment!

On the other hand, suppose that I reached only one person for Christ that first year. This time, however, I discipled him for an entire year so that he was thoroughly grounded in the Christian faith and became capable of reaching and discipling another. The next year the two of us each reached one additional person and trained those two to join us in training others. If we continued this for thirty-two years, there would be 4,294,967,296 disciples—the population of the world![4]

It's possible to have an impact on the world by investing our lives in people—yes, even junior highers!

A few years back, I had the privilege of actually seeing this process when I helped organize a staff reunion of a huge high school ministry I had been part of in the 1970s. Based on a strong disciple-making concept, the staff leaders of this ministry were committed to raising up leadership from within the group. In planning the reunion, a few friends and I decided to trace the history of this disciple-making pattern, starting with the original eight leaders in 1975 (of which I was one) and continuing through those of 1985. The results were simply staggering. We were able to trace hundreds of leaders back to these original eight. It was an incredibly sobering time when I began to realize how many people were affected directly and indirectly through our ministry. We charted out the progression on a

huge, mural-size strip of paper and placed it along a wall at the reunion. While people were milling around, I saw one young man, a member of the current team, approach Tom, one of the original leaders. With tears in his eyes, he put his arms around Tom and stated, "Tom, we've never met, but you're my spiritual great, great granddaddy." Yes, that's what disciple making is all about. Great idea: Try digging up your own spiritual roots. Once you track down your spiritual ancestors, try to contact those who are still living. Seeing you and your ministry will make their lives!

SPECIAL THANKS

It's my turn to put my words into practice and offer a sincere thanks to a few individuals who made a disciple out of me. It's a privilege to do so in front of all you readers. The faithfulness of these people helped turn a shy, insecure kid into a committed servant of God. I especially thank them for their passion—for God and for kids. I have grown to pursue that same conviction. Be proud—you did good! Thanks Marlin Duncan, Vince Valance, Ken Harrower, Ken Van Wyk, Dan Webster, Dick Dosker, and Maxine Stanton, wherever you are!

WE CAN LIVE FOREVER. Recently I've been feeling my age. My knees hurt after baseball games, and kids are starting to point out gray hairs on my head. It's only been during this past year that I've begun to seriously realize my mortality. I've also realized that I have a desperate desire to make a lasting impact on the world with my life. Disciple making allows me to do this. By investing my life in junior high kids and other faithful people, I can see my life and mission extended into the years. This excites me.

IT KEEPS US IN THE FIRE. I must confess, the older I get, the easier it becomes to create excuses for not hanging out with kids. When I commit myself to disciple-making relationships, however, it forces me to minister close up. When I see a junior higher begin to grasp the reality of Christ and how faith really means something, it makes everything I do seem worth it. Disciple making lets me be on that edge.

PUTTING IT INTO ACTION

Where do you start? Here are a few steps to help you head in the right direction.

CHOOSE A FEW FAITHFUL KIDS. Even though you're probably responsible for an entire group of kids, I encourage you to pick out a few to center on. Jesus gathered twelve, but Scripture indicates he probably focused on three (Peter, James, and John). I know it sounds like playing favorites, but if we want to have a long-lasting impact, we need to focus ourselves. Ideally, the best alternative is to develop a staff team and have each of them build disciple-making relationships with kids.

Choosing kids to focus on is a tough decision for any youth worker. The Navigators suggest this acrostic as a guide—F.A.T. (**F**aithful, **A**vailable, and **T**eachable). Go for it—search out some F.A.T. Christians.

DEVELOP A PLAN. Where would you like your kids to be spiritually by the time they leave junior high and head into high school? It's a good idea to develop a plan. Write out a list of goals that you want to see happen in kids and then set up a plan to meet those goals. While some goals are pretty general (you want every group to grasp the importance of prayer, Bible study, fellowship, and sharing the faith), other goals might be very specific to that particular group or individual. Pick up a copy of *The Ministry of Nurture: How to Build Real-Life Faith into Your Kids* by Duffy Robbins.[5] This book is an excellent tool for thinking through the disciple-making process and creating blueprints to put it into process.

SPEND TIME WITH THEM. As previously mentioned, you can't do ministry from a distance. Disciple making demands an investment of your time. First, you should spend time in a structured situation. This may mean you meet every week at a set time. Second, you should create spontaneous opportunities where you can just hang out and talk about whatever comes to mind. Ideally, you want to create a balance between both of them.

I found it wise to spend time with small groups (rather than individuals) when disciple making with junior high kids. Besides allowing you to involve a few more kids in the process, it also enables the kids to realize the power of growing close to a group of brothers and sisters. It is also wise for staff men to disciple boys and staff women to disciple girls. It makes sense in light of the obvious dangers and drawbacks, but there have been many occasions when I've had to pull aside a young staff leader and explain my reasoning.

It's fun to give your discipling group a name, and it helps create unity within the group. One ministry calls its network of discipleship groups "D-Groups." Our high school group meets at a local hamburger joint for "The Diners' Club." A friend of mine met with twelve boys who called themselves "The Dirty Dozen." My wife meets with a group of women who call themselves "The Seven Seeds." A group called "The Tennis Club" met at a local park where we studied a Christian workbook the first hour, and I taught the kids how to play tennis the second hour. One boy went on to become a youth leader *and* the top singles player on his high school tennis team—what a mentor!

In the previously mentioned book, *The Ministry of Nurture: How to Build Real-Life Faith into Your Kids*, Duffy Robbins lists a few creative ideas to spend time building disciple-making relationships, called "Thirty Things You Can Do with a Kid."[6]

1. Coke and a smile (Just sit down over a Coke).
2. Do a photo essay of other kids' rooms/or the kid's own room.
3. Make a video.
4. Throw a frisbee.
5. Throw a party.
6. Go to a professional/college sporting event.
7. Have devotions together (read Bible and pray together).
8. All night "Monopoly"/"Pictionary"/ "Trivial Pursuit" (NOTE: All night events work better with people of the same sex).
9. Go bowling.
10. Go skating.
11. Fly to Libya together.
12. Work together on a building project for Habitat for Humanity or do some other one day/one afternoon service project together.
13. Go to a school event (there's always something going on), preferably not just a popular activity. If you show up at the oboe recital, you WILL be noticed!
14. Go to a movie or rent a video.
15. Go rock climbing/hiking/cross-country skiing.
16. Ride bikes.
17. Ride zeppelins.
18. Ask the teenager to teach you how to use your computer.
19. Build a model.
20. Work on a mural for the youth room.
21. Go to the mall.
22. Set up a perfect date for the kid's friend (prepare dinner, chauffeur them around, wait on them).
23. Tutor the kid in a subject he or she is struggling with.
24. Visit a college the kid is thinking about attending.
25. Make a birthday cake for one of the other kids in the youth group.
26. Wash a car together (preferably yours; maybe theirs).
27. Practice your Boy Scout knots.
28. Work through a Bible study book together.
29. Write a song together.
30. Stay up all night and watch a meteor shower together (the best showers are after midnight).

TEACH THEM. Again, it's important to create a balance between structured and unstructured teaching times. During the structured times, it's vital to teach such issues as foundations of faith, servant-hood, faithfulness, discipline, obedience, worship, decision making, and dwelling in the presence of God . . . among others. Check out Chapter Four on creative teaching for some style options and for creative titles and additional topics.

Offering unstructured opportunities for learning is also important. Sometimes it's just getting them out of your normal structure and into a creative alternative. One summer I led a discipleship group called "Summer Servants." Every other week (we met weekly) I would take the kids to a different church. We'd interview its pastor and sit around afterward discussing what we had learned.

Look for "teachable moments." These are little windows of opportunity for teaching a principle or a truth. I can remember once being with a group of boys and noticing leaves falling off trees (no, we weren't bored). We were watching the leaves flutter to the ground when one of the boys pointed out how some came down gently while others streaked to earth in a power dive. Somehow we started talking about the Holy Spirit and how it can be ever so gentle in some circumstances and yet very powerful and dynamic in others. A great teachable moment. They're all around us, we simply need to watch for them.

ASSIGN TASKS AND DELEGATE RESPONSIBILITY. One of the central concepts of disciple making is that people we are investing in will someday invest their lives in others. Disciple making is reproductive. To accomplish this, we have to let kids take steps without us. I've seen this process explained this way: Step one, I do it and you watch; step two, I do it and you do it with me; step three, you do it and I watch; and step four, you do it and I go find another to disciple.

Delegation is scary, isn't it? Especially with junior highers. We must, however, give them the freedom to succeed or fail. Others gave us the opportunity and our kids deserve the same. Think through some of your typical responsibilities. What can you allow kids to do? You might let them help you create or lead a game, a

skit, a song, a message, or discussion questions. You could also give them a specific responsibility: edit a youth group newsletter, phone or write first-time visitors, plan an activity, set up for a meeting, or take photos.

Although I've never been the world's greatest at delegating, I am getting better. Cari, a seventh grader in one of my early junior high groups, taught me the validity of delegation in disciple making. I got to know her well when she joined a discipleship group I was coordinating one summer. Following the lesson "Being a Servant to Others," I challenged the kids to come up with some project ideas that we could do to apply what we had learned. They were supposed to think about it and report back the next week. At our next meeting I asked the kids what they came up with. Cari shared, "Steve, I have a nursing home we can visit." "Great, Cari," I answered, "maybe we can do that someday." "Well," she responded, "I've already set it up. They're expecting us next Tuesday. I'm assigning you to drive the van." I have to admit my first thoughts were to step in, take charge, and "correct" the plans she made. I'm glad I didn't. She had picked out the facility from the phone book, contacted the activities director, and set up what we would do when we got there. She had done a quality job. To her credit, that group ended up visiting that same home every month for the next three years. The kids had quite a long lasting ministry there because of Cari's vision and my willingness to let go and let her do it.

To show my improvement in this area, I asked a couple of kids I'm currently working with to create, plan, facilitate, and run a special banquet to honor all the parents in our group. They were in charge of everything. The dinner was coming up and the only thing I knew about the event was that I had to be at the church by 6:00 p.m. on Friday night. It was a little harder than I expected; delegation isn't always easy. "We had to kick Steve out of the kitchen," the kids shared, "but once he relaxed and let us run with it, everything went great!"

ENCOURAGE, ENCOURAGE, ENCOURAGE. Junior high kids need people to stick up for them and let them know they're okay. They need to hear, from us, that they're significant, capable, and able to make a difference in our world. Besides being one of the important messages of disciple making, it is also one of the joys. I get a kick out of trying to think up creative ways to encourage the kids I'm working with.

CONFRONT. Just as we must commit ourselves to encouraging, we must also be committed to confronting. Confronting someone (even a junior higher) is one of my least favorite things to do. Yet disciple making involves this act of love. I think I'd rather refer to it as "care fronting." It describes the process a little more clearly.

When I'm beginning a disciple-making relationship (with kids *and* adults), I like to sit down and have a conversation. I share with them that I'm committed to them and will back them up and give them a good report in every situation. If there's a problem, they can be assured that I will come to them directly without speaking to others. I also tell them that I want the same thing from them. This gives the relationship incredible security. When you know someone won't gossip, bad-mouth, or talk about you behind your back, you aren't threatened by confrontation.

CREATE MEMORIES. One of the healthier things we can do in a disciple-making relationship, especially with younger students like junior highers, is to create memories for them. In my adult ministry, I often reflect and draw upon my memories of being discipled by my mentors. Some of those times have become means for analyzing the effectiveness of my own ministry. I'll ask myself, "How would Ken have dealt with this situation?" or "What did Dan do when he experienced this?" Those memories give me a guide. They also help me determine what I want to develop in my own disciple-making relationships. Reproduction, after all, is what disciple making is all about.

A corny, off-the-wall . . . okay . . . creative way I try to accomplish this with the junior high kids I'm discipling is to create our own language. This might sound weird, but it helps to create a significant memory in our relationships. A young man I'm currently working with, Michael Potts, and I decided to create a word to describe something cool. We thought words like *awesome*, *incredible*, *radical*, and the like were getting a little old hat so we created the word *wad bass*. We also decided that the phrase *sad dog days* would describe a bummer, a trial, or a problem. Our goal is to try to start a new national phrase (now that the origin is published, we can prove we made it up). Okay, it's an odd process for disciple making, but hear me out. This has given Michael and me a fun way of coming to a common ground. The experience, and subsequent memory, allows us to create something that is exclusively ours. It's a special memory that will last a lifetime—a watermark to which we can point back. Twenty years from now, I want to sit down with former students of mine and reflect on those memories. Hey, disciple making is totally wad bass!

A FEW CREATIVE DISCIPLE-MAKING IDEAS

One of the fun parts of disciple making is the creativity we get to use. Understanding that the possibilities are limitless, here are a few of my favorite discipling ideas.

JOURNALING. Writing in a journal is a great way to reflect, wrestle, and think through our thoughts. Not a bad skill to teach junior highers. I like to write in little eight-by-five spiral notebooks that I buy from the corner drugstore, while my wife keeps her journal in those nice blank books that can be purchased from any stationery store. Encourage kids to keep their journals as if they were writing notes to God.

PRAYER. I want to help my kids develop a prayer life and understand that a conversation with God doesn't have to be a boring practice. I encourage them to pray through the alphabet (pray for whatever comes to mind under each letter throughout the day); pray through ACTS I (adoration, confession, thanksgiving, supplication, and intercession); or write out on a three-by-five card one or two things they want to pray for during the day and then carry the card with them.

MEMORIZE SCRIPTURE. A good mentor will try to help place Scripture on a disciple's heart. Buy the little Scripture memory cards (they come with a clear plastic holder) for your kids. Give them tunes that put Scripture to music—a great way of writing God's word on their hearts.

WORKBOOKS. Anything I can get into kids' hands that helps them think through theological issues is important to me (Bibles, books, and Christian music tapes). But my favorite is workbooks: Two great ones are *Letters to My Little Sisters* (for junior high girls)[7] and *In the Shadow of a Man* (for junior high boys).[8] Both of these workbooks come with an accompanying book.

BIBLE STUDY. A good tool for helping kids get into their Bibles is the 2 PROAPT method, developed by Chuck Miller of Barnabus Ministries: **P**ray for God's insight, **P**review the passage, **R**ead the passage, **O**bserve what it's saying, **A**pply what you learned, **P**ray for your application, and **T**ell someone what you learned.[9]

TRIPS AND RETREATS. Getting kids away gives you wonderful opportunities for nurture, growth, and disciple making (see Chapter Eight on this topic).

FINAL INSIGHT FOR THE DISCIPLE MAKER

As I write this chapter, I am reaffirming how vital disciple making is to our junior high ministries. I am being challenged myself to put the same creativity that I put into meetings, camps, and games into discipling relationships. I'm also reminded how tough disciple making can sometimes be. Maybe you can benefit from the following challenges:

THERE WILL BE DEMANDS ON OUR TIME. I once heard someone describe the spelling of *love* as "t-i-m-e." This certainly applies to disciple making. It demands a time commitment from us (something to consider before getting involved) and a time commitment from the kids. This needs to be presented clearly at the beginning of the discipleship process. For the kids' sake, we must realize that to fail to meet our commitment could do a lot of damage. For our sake, we must help the kids understand their commitment. Here's a good idea: Try writing a contract—one that acknowledges the commitment and expectations of the disciple-making process. Have the group sign it, not so much as a legalistic arrangement, but as a covenant to each other. Actually call it a covenant rather than a contract. Perhaps the covenant can be a simple verbal affirmation.

WE MAY BE HURT. This might sound like an odd thing to say, but when we pour our lives into other people, we become vulnerable. Some kids may choose to walk away from the faith; some may choose to reject you as their leader; others may fail over and over again on issues such as integrity. Whatever the case, we can't lose confidence. Remember your role and God's role in the process—you plant the seeds and God harvests the results.

LET THEM BE DIFFERENT. We must always point our kids toward Jesus. Our goal is not to make them little clones of ourselves, but disciples of Jesus. If their personalities or talents are different from our own, then we must let them run with it and become who they are. This may often mean they become better than we are in certain areas. This is a blessing, not a threat. One idea that encourages this is to expose the kids you're discipling to other leaders. This gives them examples of styles different from your own.

WE'LL RUN DRY. Like anyone else, we will go through times of spiritual drought. This is an important reason why we disciple makers need to have mentors pour their lives into *us*. Make a list. Maybe it's the senior pastor, an older youth worker, an elder, or a member in the church. You might also be encouraged by reading biographies of great spiritual leaders of the past. It's refreshing to read how these pillars of the faith wrestled with some of the same struggles we do.

You, my friends, can have an incredible impact on the world for God. You may never be on TV, negotiate with a world leader, write a book, or speak to millions, but you may change the world through the lives of others. Invest your lives in junior highers. Who knows who they will become or who they will influence in their lifetimes? Ron Lee Davis quotes a Chinese proverb with this in mind: "If you are planting for a year, plant grain. If you are planting for a decade, plant trees. If you are planting for a century, plant people."[10] Disciple making reproduces itself. High return. Smart investment!

ENDNOTES

1. Ron Lee Davis, *Mentoring: The Strategy of the Master* (Eugene, Ore.: Harvest House, 1991), 52.
2. Robert E. Coleman, *The Master Plan of Evangelism* (Old Tappan, N.J.: Revell, 1963).
3. Davis, *Mentoring*, 21.
4. Keith Phillips, *The Making of a Disciple* (Old Tappan, N.J.: Revell, 1981), 22.
5. Duffy Robbins, *The Ministry of Nurture: How to Build Real-Life Faith into Your Kids* (Grand Rapids: YS/Zondervan, 1990).
6. Robbins, *The Ministry of Nurture*, 186–87.
7. Jami Lyn Buchanan, *Letters to My Little Sisters* (Ventura, Calif.: Regal Books/Gospel Light Publications, 1984); companion workbook is by Annette Parrish and Rick Bundschuh (Ventura, Calif.: Regal Books/Gospel Light Publications, 1985).

8. Rick Bundschuh, *In the Shadow of a Man* (Ventura, Calif.: Regal Books/Gospel Light Publications, 1987); companion workbook is by Rick Bundschuh and Annette Parrish (Ventura, Calif.: Regal Books/Gospel Light Publications, 1987).

9. Chuck Miller, Barnabus Ministries, P.O. Box 1358, El Toro, CA 92630.

10. Davis, *Mentoring*, 20.

CREATIVE IDEAS FOR STUDENT MISSIONS

By Darrell Pearson

I remember clearly the first year that I ran a junior high missions trip. We were in a small town four hours from home staying in an old convent where the caretakers went to bed at 7:30 p.m.—and, of course, gave me clear guidelines concerning noise after that point. At 11:00 p.m., I had ninth graders running all over the building, three girls in tears over their combined love for the group hunk, and two boys on the roof trying to "fix" the convent bell. It's the closest I have been to packing up the troops and heading home the same night we arrived. It seemed that everyone who had cautioned me against trying missions trips with junior highers was right.

But all is not so bleak. There are great missions ideas and opportunities available for junior high students. With some thought and direction, you can offer kids the joy of service through creative student missions.

STUDENTS IN SERVICE

The point of using junior highers in service and missions is not so much that the world needs their skills and help, but that *they* need the personal experience to better understand their faith. In the process of doing something for someone else, they are given a glimpse of God's role for them in their world. And in the process of helping, they often actually accomplish something constructive.

When designing service opportunities, be prepared for most adults to give you a negative response. Senior citizens often are hesitant to let kids work on their homes, and faraway missions are petrified of junior highers creating more messes than the messes they came to clean up. One pastor at a Navajo reservation church asked me on the phone, "What work projects have your kids done at *your* church?" Good question! So we start with service ideas close to home.

RELATIONAL SERVICE OPPORTUNITIES

There is no better local missions for junior high kids than visiting nursing homes and shut-ins. In fact, I'm always shocked at how few kids hesitate to sit and chat with old people. Kids have fewer hangups than adults concerning the imminent future. I have to struggle with the reality that I'm halfway home! Junior highers are great at just visiting with the elderly. Don't think they have to entertain all the time, either. You don't need a choir to go to a nursing home. You can just take kids and let them be themselves and visit. Seniors think they're wonderful!

My feeling is that the best service opportunities for junior highers always involve something relational. It's not enough to just do work; they have to have a connection with somebody. Local relief agencies are great places for kids to help, but don't let the adults lock them in the kitchen stirring the soup. Students need to be challenged by dishing up that soup to real people.

Some of my students recently cooked a meal for people staying at our local Ronald McDonald house (where parents and siblings of a child in the hospital can stay during the hospitalization). Cooking the food was fun, but the experience reached its fulfillment in the delivery of that food. The kids were confronted with the reality of families in struggle, and they helped to comfort and ease the pain a little bit. It was the relational part that made it work.

This is not to say that kids should not do specific tasks, but make sure a relational experience is a part of every service opportunity. Picking up trash on the highway fulfills a community need, but where is the relational aspect? Make it a part of every mission.

IN-HOUSE OPPORTUNITIES

Although there is a terrific amount of enthusiasm for the faraway missions project, service opportunities abound at home. You may have to take your group on the exotic missions adventure just to get them excited about serving, but helping on the home front will be where most groups will—and should—grow a heart for serving others. There are many areas of local opportunities available for the creative youth worker who looks for them.

My junior high group is always asked to help with projects that the adult Sunday school classes want to overlook. A few months ago our church received new Bibles for the pews but it soon became apparent that many of the pages were missing. The church needed someone to go through every Bible and look for the misprinted copies. Predictably, the adults wouldn't do it, but it took ten seconds of recruiting to find fifteen volunteers who completed the project in forty-five minutes. There are always envelopes to stuff, driveways to sweep, and walkways to shovel. Certainly your church has some projects that no one else wants to do. Unfortunately, the relational aspect of these tasks is low, but there is some built-in meaning, since the kids are tied into their own church and its facility. It also helps to have adults working with them so that they have to relate to others while they work.

Helping out with younger children is an area where junior highers can really shine. Although they always have to be supervised, they have the energy and the ability to work with kids that often the appointed adults can't seem to find. My five-year-old daughter attends a Sunday school class where the junior highers are really the key helpers (incidentally, the class meets at a different hour than the junior high Sunday school). They are the ones she talks about on the way home and who seem to really care about her. I know the adults are there and that they put in most of the prep time, but the eighth and ninth graders working with the kids add a terrific excitement and interest level.

In addition to Sunday school, many churches have programs for day-care kids, latchkey children, recreation, Vacation Bible School, and nurseries, all of which offer some opportunities for junior highers to contribute. Junior highers are good helpers in music and drama, particularly doing a superb job with puppets and stories. Always be careful to meet legal standards for adult supervisors, but don't hesitate to involve junior highers in the lives of younger students. They often are the most motivated and enthusiastic helpers in the church.

When my wife and I call for a babysitter, we usually try to secure a junior high student. High schoolers are great—they are more mature in many ways, but it's the junior high people who work the hardest to be good sitters. They don't just sit and watch the tube or talk on the phone, they play hard with the kids. They'll do the same at church helping out in the children's areas.

Sometimes the junior high student who is bored with everything needs a new challenge. Tutoring younger students is very fulfilling for them, and a great help to elementary students struggling in a specific area. Since the older student is in the midst of being educated, they often

have a solid grasp of the curren the younger kids are trying to stand. One-on-one tutoring is a ben both the helper and the helpee.

WORK, WORK, WORK

I will never forget the work trip I to with some kids where I was excited abo a one-to-three adult-to-junior-highe ratio. I knew we would be able to accom plish a lot of really quality work. During one twenty-minute period, I left three reliable girls in a bathroom of the home we were painting, leaving specific instructions to paint everything in the room white. Of course, I didn't mean *every*thing, but that is precisely what the young ladies did. Not only were the walls white, but so were the faucets and the tile! They took my instructions quite literally. It seemed obvious to me what to do, but no one had told them specifically what was expected.

Junior highers need clear instructions. They are capable of doing quality work when an adult has led them step-by-step through each detail. A short seminar on how to paint—brush strokes, not too much paint on the brush, taping edges— was helpful for kids inexperienced in basic work skills. If you are doing construction, such as rebuilding a fence, use extreme care when using tools. I have noticed that junior high boys don't mind trading off with hand tools when power tools are unavailable. It takes longer to do the job, but it's safer.

Sometimes you'll have kids who have a specific skill already developed from working at home or from shop class. An eighth grader on a recent work trip had helped his dad build a wall in the basement; he became the work foreman.

When it comes to painting, many students are good with detail work but paint poorly over a large area. Some junior high girls once painted flowers on the trim of a small Mexican house we were building, and the neighbors came over to ask them to do *their* houses as well. The girls ended up painting flowers all over the neighborhood, and the flowers looked good! Use the skills and interests the kids already have.

This is why yard work, with the exception of lawn mowing, doesn't always go over too well. Puttering around the yard is not a big interest for junior high students. I have had few successes with yard work and cleaning; it seems the kids lose patience quickly with the projects and don't do a very good job.

The best work project we ever had was a request to demolish a building. On a trip to New Mexico, two students were assigned the task of tearing down an old adobe house with two-foot thick walls. We didn't think they would make much headway, but Alex and Sarah proved us wrong. Two adults stood and supervised to make sure the project was safe while these two students got into it. When it was time to break for lunch and escape the searing heat, the two kids ate a quick snack and returned to the scene of the crime. Within two days, the house was three-fourths gone. It was a perfect marriage—junior highers and destruction! You probably won't find many demolition projects available, but if you do, grab them.

Here are a few other wild ideas for missions projects.

SPONSOR A FREE CAR WASH. You are not raising money for anything, just doing something nice for others.

HAVE A CANNED FOOD OR A CLOTHING DRIVE. Collect only certain items. For example, our local downtown ministry needed underwear to hand out to families with clothing needs. We held a "brief" drive to collect the necessary items. It was needed, and it was "junior highish."

SPONSOR A COMPASSION CHILD. For $21.00 a month, you can sponsor a child. Put several students in charge of collecting the offering each month and motivating the others. Compassion's address is P.O. Box 7000, Colorado Springs, CO 80933.

HOLD A DANCE FOR THE SENIOR CITIZENS OF YOUR CHURCH. It can be a square dance or a formal setting with a band. Have the kids pay for it and prepare the refreshments.

PUT ON PLAYS. Perform plays for children's programs at church and in your city. Have the kids write a puppet theater production and do it for local daycare programs.

GET INVOLVED WITH LOCAL DISABLED MINISTRIES AND PROGRAMS. Call to find out how your kids can be involved in these ministries. Just spending time with handicapped kids, playing basketball and games, and taking walks is a boost for both parties.

Have the same disabled kids visit your Sunday or midweek program. Their presence will add a new dimension to the program. (We once had a group home that brought their students to Sunday classes each week; it was not unusual for one of them to scream out in the middle of the lesson. It was uncomfortable but was soon accepted by the mainstream kids.)

Or have a handicapped night when nondisabled kids have to do relays in wheelchairs, play soccer blindfolded with a blind-ball, or read backward looking in a mirror.

GO CAROLING. Avoid the Christmas rush. Go caroling at a nursing home at Easter, in midsummer, or at Thanksgiving.

WRITE LETTERS TO NONATTENDING KIDS. Check the kids' letters so that they don't say anything too foolish!

WRITE LETTERS TO OVERSEAS MISSIONARIES. Many missionaries never hear from anyone back home. A junior higher's sense of humor and writing style will be refreshing to them.

DO LOCAL, ONGOING MINISTRIES. Get involved in a local ministry that your kids can be a part of on an ongoing basis. Playing with the kids of a resettled Soviet family could be a once-a-month ministry.

BE HOSPITAL HELPERS. Suggest that kids become summer candy stripers at a hospital.

RAISE FUNDS FOR OTHERS. Call the local hospice (they work with terminally ill patients) and see if they have a fund-raising event your group can help with.

RAISE MONEY FOR A ONE-TIME PROJECT. Missions needs that require ongoing funds are tough for junior highers. They need to work at meeting one need and goal at a time.

INVITE SPEAKERS INTO YOUR GROUP. Invite a missionary on furlough who is visiting your congregation to a junior high activity. Don't have them show slides. Just let the kids get to know them as real people.

SERVICE TRIPS

Many would shy away from service trips with junior high students, but I think it's a valid way for kids to experience what missions and service is all about. Some guidelines help make the experience worthwhile and well run.

Note the following cautions, though: Don't take kids on a service trip unless they are already doing service at home on a regular basis. Don't take kids you feel would cause problems in a strange culture or there may be serious discipline issues. Also, I wouldn't take junior highers on a trip that is beyond the scope of their understanding, such as the poverty found in Haiti. Leave something for their high school years.

TYPES OF TRIPS

Service trips don't have to be just work related. You can have a very profitable time doing something besides building.

MISSIONS EDUCATION TRIPS. Visiting and interviewing people at specific missions can be very worthwhile. The students learn what a commitment to missions means, and they have the chance to catch a brief glimpse of the big picture.

VACATION BIBLE SCHOOLS. Putting together and leading a local VBS has a lot of merit. It adds the relational experience I talked about earlier and gives kids a hands-on approach to service. It also adds a unique spiritual dimension, since kids are sharing their faith with others.

WORK TRIPS. These trips offer students the chance to build, clean, or paint. If done well and appropriately, they can be very meaningful for junior highers.

Finding an appropriate junior high project is always a tough task. As mentioned earlier, many missions locations are not open to junior highers coming for a visit, much less doing a building project. It takes some serious research, mainly on the telephone, to find and convince someone you have a valid idea. Try writing one of these agencies for ideas.

1. *Amor Ministries*, 1664 Precision Park Lane, San Diego, CA 92073.
2. *Compassion International*, P.O. Box 7000, Colorado Springs, CO 80933.
3. *Group's Junior High Service Trips*, 2890 Monroe Avenue So., Loveland, CO 80539.
4. *World Servants*, 160 Harbor Drive, Key Biscayne, FL 33149.
5. *Teen Missions International*, P.O. Box 1056, Merritt Island, FL 32952.
6. Your denominational missions department.

Don't undertake a project that is too extensive for junior high students. I have found that junior highers can effectively work around five hours a day, three days maximum. After building a tradition and traveling with experienced kids, these maximums can be extended. The weather plays a part. If it is too hot where you are, kids won't work well.

Adequate planning makes all the difference.

VISIT YOUR DESTINATION. If possible, visit your destination so that you've met the hosts, have seen the site, know the accommodations, and have prepared the people the kids will be spending time with to know what's coming. Last summer I visited our trip's missions church a day early to make sure the work site was properly prepared. The local Mexican pastor had done an excellent job of laying a concrete foundation for the nursery we were to build, but his dimensions were four inches off my plans. I needed to know that so that I could adjust my calculations to meet his foundation.

Making adequate arrangements for food and shelter is a necessity, too. The health of your junior high kids is a paramount concern. Don't compromise their safety for issues of cultural awareness. It's all they can do to handle the mental adjustment of a new place and demands without having to handle a culinary change as well.

EDUCATE YOUR STUDENTS. Before you leave, teach your kids about the place you're going. A videotape concerning Navajo cultural issues was helpful for me before a trip into Arizona. Bible studies on the biblical approach to missions and service are invaluable. Skill development to learn how to build your project is helpful. Hold a practice work day to determine which kids have the commitment and the desire to be accepted for this trip.

HOLD PARENT MEETINGS. Prior to the trip, have a parent meeting to alleviate concerns, answer questions, and help the parents determine your reliability and trustworthiness. One friend of mine had a second parent meeting prior to the students' return, to prepare the parents for the changes that may have occurred in their kids.

PREPARE A HANDOUT ABOUT THE TRIP. Trip details, such as where you're staying each night, emergency phone numbers where parents can reach you, an itinerary of each day's activities, and a list of adult leadership all help ensure that the trip will go smoothly.

BE ORGANIZED. An organized work project will certainly help. I have found that I need to break kids down into specific task groups with clear instructions for the leader. For example, for the trip mentioned above, three kids were assigned to saw two-by-fours to the proper length, groups of six kids each were to build specific walls, and one group of kids was assigned to play basketball with the local children!

Service and missions trips are not easy

to run, but they are enormously worthwhile. While working in Mexico several years ago, some ninth grade girls discovered a sick and dying dog in the corner of an abandoned house near where we were working. They desperately wanted to do something for him, but they couldn't. They had to come to grips with the reality of the dog's situation, which gave them an understanding, in a small way, of the predicament of many of the people we were serving.

THE FAMILY WORK TRIP

If the standard work and service trip seems beyond possibility or interest, try the family work trip. We've had great success running a five-day work experience for families during spring break. It almost becomes part vacation and part work trip, because the families have so much fun working, playing, cooking, sightseeing, joking, and shopping together. The parents give you built-in discipline with their kids, and every parent is given the right to straighten out others when necessary. Families rotate cooking assignments, and discussions are held both within their own family groups and by forming new families. Our groups have worked on Habitat for Humanity homes. We had a great time, and we were able to accomplish a lot of work, partly because we had such a strong kid-to-adult ratio. During the week, families get some space: a day to shop or sightsee on their own, or we travel back home independently. We have even taken some kids with other families on a short-term "adoption" for the week. I have been amazed at the response of many people to this trip and at the incredible diversity of family types attending. It's a great change from the usual!

WRAPPING IT UP

Junior highers and missions . . . they belong together. Don't let other adults convince you that a seventh grader can't serve others. They not only want to, they need to, and given the opportunity you provide them, they will see the world in a different and life-changing way.

of the games don't require specific athletic skill. This is obviously a big deal to nonathletes. The church can be a safe place where kids can be free from the pressure that comes from winning or losing.

I encourage you to pick up a copy of the book *Play It! Great Games for Groups* by Wayne Rice and Mike Yaconelli.[1] This book is an excellent collection of games that can be used regardless of ability or skill.

CREATING YOUR OWN GREAT GAMES

Who says that we always have to play the standard games? Some of the best games you can use are the ones that you create. Here are a few hints on getting started.

ADD A TOUCH OF THE OUTRAGEOUS. A few years ago, while leading recreation for a large high school camp in San Diego, I organized a wild game called "Total Mass Confusion" for one of the evening sessions. Each of the 700 kids were given a sheet that listed twenty crazy things to do. Some of the tame ones included "find twenty people and sing the *Gilligan's Island* theme song," "build a pyramid with a group of strangers," and "form a train with forty people and weave around the room barking like dogs." At the starting whistle, the room was transformed into a madhouse as kids ran everywhere performing the bizarre, off-the-wall antics. It was an amazing scene.

It was even more amazing to watch the reaction of some of the adult leaders. With a somewhat nervous, scared look, a few leaders were running around trying to stop kids from going crazy. They didn't understand the concept of the activity.

While I saw healthy ministry happening in the outrageous game, they only saw what they perceived as kids "out of control." There's a big difference between being outrageous and being out of control. A successful junior high leader knows the difference. We have become wise in knowing just how much of the reins can be let out without losing control. Many adults only know how to keep the reins in close. It is no wonder that kids are overjoyed with bizarreness in our games. Don't be shy in letting your creativity run rampant. It will make some adults nervous, but awesome games can result. After all, we *all* have to be a little outrageous to work with junior highers.

USE YOUR IMAGINATION. Remember when you were a child and you spent hours entertaining yourself with your imagination? You and your friends came up with the greatest games to occupy your afternoons, weekends, and summer days. I believe that you still have that ability. Sure, your imagination may be a bit rusty, but with a little work you can do it. Here are a few tips that I use to get my imagination geared for coming up with my most creative games.

• **Use common objects:** Walk around your church looking for odd objects to build a game around. It's amazing what you can do with the stuff you find on the property (our kids loved bobsledding down a ramp on a roller our custodian uses to stack chairs). Get a few ideas by just walking around the office. Try using empty plastic containers from the water cooler as bowling pins or use the rolling office chairs for a relay race in which the kids get pushed around. One youth worker I know gets game ideas from objects he finds behind stores. He also finds some pretty unusual giveaway prizes.

• **Walk through toy stores:** Browse around a toy store. Besides being a fun thing to do, it's also a great way of coming up with game ideas. Toy manufacturers are always thinking up hot new ideas that become great catalysts for our own use. It's amazing what you can do with Play-doh, silly putty, and Hula-Hoops. Speaking of Hula-Hoops, I recently picked up a few from a toy store for an event. We tried to see how many kids we could stuff in one, had kids jump through them into a pile of pillows, and used them as giant rings for a ring toss game. Oh yeah, we also spun them around our waists. Novel idea, huh?

• **Reconstruct traditional games:** During my college years, I worked for my city as a recreation leader. I was always needing to come up with creative games. I discovered that by taking traditional games (football, baseball, basketball) and rearranging them a bit, I could create some pretty fun activities. Some examples of this include playing baseball with a racquetball racket and a whiffleball, playing football while hopping on one foot, and playing volleyball with a giant beach ball. The possibilities are awesome when you simply vary the rules.

• **Ask the group to come up with ideas:** A few years ago, I took our junior highers to the mountains for what I called an "uncamp." This was simply a retreat with few plans. During the afternoon, I was amazed at the creative games the kids came up with when I told them I hadn't planned anything specific for them. Left alone, they were awesome in their inventions. I really shouldn't have been so surprised. Kids are experts at games. A wise youth worker will listen to them.

• **Watch TV:** Some of the greatest game ideas can be found right on the television set. Not only can we gather ideas from shows, cartoons, and commercials, we can also simulate popular game shows. I'm always doing this. Sometimes we'll play the game just like the TV version and other times we'll add all sorts of variances. This winter I built a big spinning wheel out of cardboard, placed letters on a wall, and played *Wheel of Fortune.* I even used it for memorizing Bible verses.

• **Look at a book:** There are many books available that list all sorts of games and recreation ideas. Look through these books and adapt some of the ideas to fit your own needs. You may want to collect a few of these books by having your church buy them for you to use. Most libraries have game books. Still short on ideas? Give your city parks and recreation department a call. You could even contact the physical education department at your local school for ideas.

• **Balance the elaborate with the simple:** It's great fun pulling off elaborate game events (actually, I get most of the fun out of just dreaming them up). For twelve thematic game nights (one for each month), check out *Junior High Game Nights* by Dan McCollam and Keith Betts.[2] It's also important to realize that simplicity has its benefits. You can do a lot with a little. Modern playground design reflects this belief. It seems that a Danish landscape architect commissioned to rebuild playgrounds that were damaged during World War II found that children preferred to play in the bombed out rubble rather than in the new parks he had developed.[3] Don't sweat it if you don't have the resources for the elaborate. With a little creativity, the kids will enjoy whatever you've got.

THE RIGHT GAME AT THE RIGHT TIME

It's said that there's a time and a place for everything. This includes game times. I've seen some of the best programs ruined because games were poorly prepared, poorly chosen, or poorly timed. While there's a place for spontaneous recreation, there's also a place for the right game—at the right time. Here are some factors to consider when choosing, preparing, and timing your recreation and games.

PROGRAM OBJECTIVE. If a game is wrapped in an event where it precedes or follows another activity (a skit, singing, a talk), it's essential that the game works in sync with the rest of the program. Games and recreation should complement a program rather than distract from it. In light of this, it's important to have a program objective and know where the game fits in. If the game is at the beginning of a weekly meeting, it should probably be high energy to let the kids get their "rowdies" out. If the game is preceding a talk, it should be low energy (unless you have a wild speaker) to help the kids settle and focus.

SPACE CONSIDERATIONS. *Where* you play is obviously an important factor in choosing a game. If you're inside, consider the floor (hard or soft), the surroundings (can we break anything?), the height of the ceiling, the noise factor (is there a women's prayer group meeting next door?), and the size of the room. If you're outside, consider the weather, boundaries (will we lose balls or kids?), light (how long until dark?), and neighbors (is there anyone we could disturb . . . are they big and mean . . . do they donate to the church?).

TIME CONSIDERATIONS. It's important to know how much time you have to play your game. Don't forget to include the explanation of the rules and take any questions during this time. It's also wise to set up as much of the game as possible in advance. Think through boundaries and rules, and have all the props and equipment laid out. I make a habit of playing the game (actual or in my mind) beforehand. This helps me understand how much time is needed for the game and helps me anticipate glitches to be prepared with alternatives. Hint: I always have a game or two up my sleeve in case I have some time to fill.

GROUP SIZE. Some games are only meant for small or large groups. Simple anticipation should make this decision easy. The good news is that whether you have two or 2,000, there is a game for your group. If you don't know how many kids you'll have, then it's probably smart to have several game options.

SEX OF THE GROUP. Certain games are better suited for same-sex groups than others. Although both boys and girls are capable of playing the same games (even the hard hitting ones), a little wisdom is needed to determine whether to have them play it together. If I am playing a rough game with boys and girls, I will often adjust the rules to even out the competition. For example, our kids love to play "Flamingo Football," where the boys have to play the entire game while hopping on one foot. The girls get to play normally. They usually drill the boys.

CLOTHING CONSIDERATIONS. There have been quite a few instances in which I had to change a game at the last minute because most of the girls were wearing dresses. This was unusually poor planning on my part. If I am planning a game that requires a certain type of clothing, I now make sure the kids know in advance.

GROUP PERSONALITY. Chances are that some of my kids' favorite games would go over like a lead balloon in your group. Why? Every group has its own personality. When you consider games, you have to take this into consideration and try to match the activity with the group. There are, however, instances where it's good to throw something at them if their personality needs to be shaken up a bit. If the group is lethargic, then perhaps it needs a high energy game. If it's borderline out of control, then maybe a low energy game is in order.

SEASON. I'm lucky—I live in an area of the country where I can snow ski in mountains, surf at the beach, or ride dune buggies in the desert—all in one day! Recreation in Los Angeles certainly isn't limited by seasons. This isn't true for many of you. The games you choose may be more appropriate in some seasons than others. This is determined easily enough. Note: Sometimes it's fun to mix them up and play games out of season—volleyball in the snow or sledding in the summer (using ice blocks on grass).

EQUIPMENT AND PROPS

Each year, at the end of March, I get to go shopping for toys. This is the time of year (prior to the expiration of my current year's budget) that I've set aside for purchasing new recreation and game equipment. It's a really fun adventure. I get to wander through sporting goods and toy stores, picking out all sorts of odds and ends for our youth ministry. Believe me when I say this is one of my most favorite times of the year.

Although I am committed to buying recreation equipment for our group, I really don't spend an outrageous amount of money. I actually collect much of our equipment from garage sales and church family discards. It's a great way of picking up worn but useful equipment. My creative ability often enables me to come up with some use for almost any item. I was recently given a frame and netting that was once a backyard backstop for hitting golf balls. After a little creative reworking, I was able to turn the unit into two goals for playing street hockey.

To store all our equipment, I have designated a large closet that I call the "toy box." The care and storage of any recreation equipment is important if you want it to last and stick around. To avoid disappearance, inventory and mark all items. Also, require that everything is checked out through the secretary. Some of your more valuable equipment should be placed under lock and key. Note: I'm very aware that recreation equipment is meant to be used. It's a wasted ministry tool if it sits in a closet. Therefore, I try to be free with our items. Equipment will be broken and lost; it's part of the game.

Here is a list of equipment that is a good starter set for a junior high group serious about having game and recreation activities. Some are important, some are not. Dream a bit and list what you would like to have.

STARTER RECREATION EQUIPMENT LIST

Support Equipment
Ball pump/needles
Whistle
Ball bag
Clipboard
Stopwatch

First aid kit
Cones
Air horn
Rope
Line marker (lime)
Pens and pencils
Scratch paper

Balls

Rubber playground ball
Football
Basketball
Volleyball
Softball
Baseball
Soccer ball
Beach balls
Tennis balls
Racquetball
Whiffleball
Ping-Pong balls
Foam (nerf) ball
Incredible ball (cloth)
Giant push ball

Miscellaneous

Bases
Softball bat
Whiffleball bat
Volleyball net
Frisbees
Soccer goals
Football belt flags
Street hockey sticks/pucks/balls
Smashball paddles/balls
Tennis rackets
Racquetball rackets
Brooms (broomball, hockey)
Hula-Hoops
Croquet set
Squirt guns
Water balloons/launcher
Dart board
Replacement parts

Board Games

"Pictionary"
"Outburst"
"Balderdash"
"Twenty-one Questions"
"Adverteasing"
"Scattergories"
"Trivial Pursuit"
"Ungame"
Bingo
"Twister"
Chess
Checkers
TV game show home games
Bible Trivia

Odds and Ends

Kite and string
TV theme song albums
Camera
Measuring tape
Clothespins
Prizes
Old magazines
Poster paper
Marker pens
Chalk
Portable chalkboard
Lantern/flashlight
Megaphone
Plastic tarps
Clean-up supplies
Calculator
Wood table games
Trash cans

Add Your Own List

TYPES OF GAMES

As I mentioned before, there's a game for almost every situation. Let's take a look at some game categories and a few of my favorite options.

TEAM GAMES. Teams are great for organization. This is especially helpful if you have a larger group. One of my favorites is a game called "Bottom Ball." Similar to basketball, this game is played on . . . well . . . your bottom. Behind each team is a trash can serving as the basket. The object is to make "baskets" in the other team's trash can without leaving your bottoms (our kids call it TBC—that means **T**otal **B**un **C**ontact). Cones are placed around each can to prevent dunks. We play with five to ten balls (depending upon the size of the group) so there is a lot of action. Referees behind each can count the baskets and throw balls back into the playing area.

RELAY GAMES. My all-time favorite relay is the "Sleeping Bag Relay." Each person puts a sleeping bag over his or her head and body. The kids then run out to a marker and back. The results are hilarious to watch. The "Bat Spin Relay" is another good one. This classic has each person run to a baseball bat, place her or his forehead on the bat (with the other end on the ground), spin around a designated number of times, and return to his or her line. A little dizzy, the kids returning to the line are a riot to watch.

ELIMINATION GAMES. These games eliminate participants until only the winner remains. Make sure these games are entertaining to watch since you'll have, at some point, a large number of kids on the sidelines. One of my favorites is called "Toe Fencing." Everyone in the group pairs up, partners lock wrists (or take hands), and attempt to step on the other's feet without having theirs stepped on. The winner pairs up with another winner, while the losers are eliminated.

This goes on until there are only two left. Put music on while the kids are playing. It looks like everyone is dancing.

QUIET GAMES. Quiet games are good as a warm-up for Sunday school, for a meeting in someone's home, to precede a serious moment, for a location where you can't be loud, or for a time when the group is mellow and not in a wild mood. A great quiet game (and full of laughs) is "Dictionary." A form of this game is being retailed by The Games Gang, Ltd. as "Balderdash." Your props are a dictionary, pencils, and paper. One person comes up with an outrageous word (one that no one knows the definition of). The word is said out loud and everyone writes out his or her best bluff definition on paper, signs it, and turns it in. The lead person reads all the definitions out loud (including the real one) and everyone guesses which is the correct one. Points are given as follows: One point for guessing the correct definition, two points for having someone guess your bluff, and three points to the lead person if no one guesses the correct answer. Each person or group rotates being the lead person with the dictionary. My staff loves playing this game!

LARGE AREA GAMES. Usually played outdoors, these games require lots of room and lots of time. This type of game is excellent at camp. My favorite wild game is actually any variation around the classic game "Capture the Flag." The group divides into two teams. Each side has a flag in the rear of its territory, surrounded by a few feet of free space. Each team also has a jail area. The objective is to get the other team's flag back to your side without being caught (tagged). Once you cross into enemy territory, you can be tagged and sent to jail, only being released when a player from your team is able to tag you. Note: Create rules to keep the game running smoothly. Kids everywhere love this popular game. There's something thrilling about sneaking around and trying not to be caught (no wonder junior high kids like it so much). Add little variations to this game, like playing at night with the flags being lanterns or having the staff equipped with water balloons and flour (heh, heh).

MIXING GAMES. These are simply games that mix kids. They're ideal for opening a meeting, loosening up a crowd, or helping a group get to know each other. One of my favorites, "Total Mass Confusion," was described earlier in this chapter. Another classic is the "Name Game." The name of a famous personality (Elvis, Cleopatra, Mr. Ed, Steve Dickie) is written on paper and taped to the back of each kid. The kids wander around and try to guess who their person is by asking "yes" and "no" questions. Another favorite of my group's is "Clothespin Mania." A pile of clothespins is dumped in the center of the room. The objective is to pin clothespins to others' clothing without getting pinned yourself. Fun times!

VISUAL GAMES. Fun to play, these games are even more fun to watch. They work well when you call a representative from each team and the group cheers for them. I call one of my favorites the "Big Yank" game. Place two small one-to-three foot tall platforms (chairs work fine) about five feet apart. Two kids stand on each platform facing each other. Each holds an end of a rope. The objective is to pull the other off of the platform by yanking on the rope. Strategy comes into play when you let out and bring in the rope to where your opponent is at the end of his or her rope. Set up wild obstacle courses,

either in a room or outside. Kids love to watch others do crazy stuff. You can have them do some of the wackiest things imaginable—use your imagination.

WATER GAMES. These games use . . . uh . . . water. Be wise in your timing of these type of games. You don't want kids wet when it's cold or when they have to sit in damp clothing for a while. Try the "Bucket Game." The group is divided into two or more teams; each has a plastic trash can in its team area. Each team member is given a paper cup. The objective is to see which team can fill its trash can the quickest, using only paper cups. The water can come from anywhere—drinking fountains, swimming pools, or toilets. A fun (and wild) variation is to let the team members prevent opposing team members from getting water to the trash can.

SPORTS AND ATHLETICS

A few words should be said about this topic. I'm a firm believer that sports have a great place in the life of a church, especially in youth ministry. They are a very positive way to have fun, create team unity, teach healthy competition, rally kids, and reach out to students who might normally never come near a church.

One of the many things that hooked me into the youth group where I became a Christian was the fact that they played competitive sports on Sunday afternoons. I loved it. I'm sure there were some kids who weren't interested in that kind of activity, but I (and many of the friends I brought) was attracted by it. We'd play softball in spring, football in fall, basketball in winter, and volleyball in summer. I recall that the church custodian made us soccer goals when he saw us playing soccer one afternoon. I thought that was so cool. I also admired those great adults who came out to play hard with us kids.

I guess I've never forgotten the influence that sports had on my coming to know Jesus because I use it frequently in my ministry today. Here are a few things I do.

SPORT LEAGUES. I love to get our kids involved in leagues. Organizing one isn't that difficult. I call a couple of neighborhood churches with junior high groups and set one up. Hint: Call a youth worker at a church with a gym, ask if they want to be in a league, and then tell them it will be at their place! Besides such activities as softball, football, basketball, and bowling, we once organized a very competitive indoor soccer league.

TOURNAMENTS. If a full league is out of the question, then a one-day tournament is often the answer. Our kids have really gotten into street hockey, so I am currently organizing a tourney with other churches. Kids from our high school group are going to referee.

CHALLENGES. This is an easy way to organize something—challenge another group to a game. I have even challenged our high school group and occasionally our college group to events. Yes, we often win against the high school kids. In 1984, our junior high boys even defeated our college guys consecutively in softball and soccer (they didn't like that too much and I've never let them forget it).

JUST-SHOW-UP TIMES. Designate times where your kids know that some activity is planned. All they have to do is show up and play. This is great on Sunday afternoons, Saturday nights, or even after school. Playing after school, at the school, allows for a great outreach opportunity as you gather kids to play.

COACHING. This isn't exactly with your church kids, but it's a great way to meet kids and get involved with the community. Try volunteering to coach a junior high level sport. The schools and youth athletic organizations would probably go crazy over someone like you. I have also found that the parents love you, too. Because of your work with the church (sure, it makes some nervous), they are thankful to have someone of integrity spending time with their kids.

A FEW FINAL HELPFUL HINTS

1. Play fair.
2. Don't show favoritism.
3. Know when to end a game.
4. Know when to extend a game.
5. Be willing to dump a game that isn't working.
6. Have game options up your sleeve.
7. Don't ever embarrass a kid.
8. Don't call down kids or leaders in front of the group.
9. Encourage.
10. Think through the game before you play it.
11. Have all the equipment and props ready before you play.
12. Don't be afraid to cheer, yell, and get into it.
13. Flow.
14. Be outrageous and bizarre.
15. Think through hazards, dangers, and safety before playing.
16. Consider what your game is teaching.
17. Know which activity follows your game.
18. Understand the needs of your group.
19. Add variety.
20. Play safe.

Above all, make sure that *you* have fun. If the kids know that you're having a blast playing hard, they will enjoy your weird, wild, and outrageous games even more. After all, you're just a big junior higher, aren't you? Minister hard and love kids hard, but don't forget to play hard!

ENDNOTES

1. Wayne Rice and Mike Yaconelli, *Play It! Great Games for Groups* (Grand Rapids: YS/Zondervan, 1986).
2. Dan McCollam and Keith Betts, *Junior High Game Nights* (Grand Rapids: YS/Zondervan, 1991).
3. Anonymous, "Get Dirty, Have Fun: That's the Adventure Playground Idea," *Sunset* 186, no. 6 (June 1991): 20.

DARRELL'S TWENTY-SIX INCREDIBLY HOT PROGRAM IDEAS AND TIPS

1. **THE TABLE GAME:** Find one of those classic "church" tables (folding rectangular—every church has about three million) and set it up in front of the group. Have a person sit on top of the table, then try to climb over the side, under the table, and back up the other side—without touching the ground, the table legs, or the supports. It usually takes a gymnast to do it. Great game to use as a filler when your talk on "small yellow plants of the Bible" is dying.

2. **NOTES AND PHOTOS**: Junior highers love mail—everybody knows that. So how many postcards have you written lately? Don't just write a note; include a photo you took of the student long jumping at his or her track meet.

3. **INTRODUCTION TO JUNIOR HIGH NIGHT**: Have a parents' night for just the incoming sixth

graders' parents (or fifth) to introduce them to the wild world of junior high life. Tell them about your philosophy, what you're like as a person, and why you do what you do. Show some slides of great activities, and have several older students share how they survived the experience.

4. **LEG WRESTLING**: It's old, but it works well as a fill-in. Pair up everybody in the room, then wrestle off until you have a champion. You'll be surprised who wins. While you're at it, have a girls' arm wrestling contest. The results here will also surprise you.

5. **MAKEUP KIT**: Keep a makeup kit handy with some simple face paints in bright colors, a wig, and so on. You never know when, at a moment's notice, you need to look like the Joker.

6. **PIZZA DELIVERY**: Call up three different pizza companies at the same time and see which one delivers to your junior high room first. After they all make it, have a taste test to determine the winner.
7. **WRITE-ON SLIDES**: This activity works well with young junior highers. Buy some blank write-on slides at the photo store, hand out pens, and let kids do their own thing on the slides. After fifteen minutes of colorful creations, rack them up in a slide tray and show them on the wall with a song playing in the background.
8. **LIFESTYLES OF THE POOR AND OBSCURE**: If you have a video camera, go to a student's house during the day and film the kid's room, the dog, baby pictures on the wall, and so on. Interview his or her dad about the kid's "intricacies." Do your best Robin Leach impression, then announce on Sunday that the midweek program will feature one of *them*.
9. **FAITH MONUMENTS**: Never be afraid to create a big moment in a kid's life. The weekly lesson is fine, Bible study is great, but kids need that big jolt once in a while to give them memory keepsakes of their growth in the Lord. Sunrise watching after a middle-of-the-night hike, the classic camp commitments, a play for the whole church, the sharing of a testimony—all these give kids something they can really remember.
10. **PHOTO BOOK**: Run a master list of your group, leaving enough room after each name for a photo. This is particularly helpful for big groups. A new adult volunteer can become familiar with the kids even before he or she meets them. The leader who "just can't remember that kid's name" can use the reinforcement.
11. **REQUIRING A PHOTO**: On the same topic, require that kids submit a recent photo when they turn in their retreat registration. This not only gives you a jump in the relationship development market, but it helps you compile your photo book.
12. **AWARDS CEREMONY**: After any significant event, trip, or graduation party, give away awards based on outstanding performances. Make sure every kid's name gets mentioned. For extra laughs, tie their achievement to a current movie or TV title.
13. **GRAB BAG GAME**: Take an ordinary paper grocery bag, fold over the top (inside) about two inches, set it on the floor, then, one by one, ask the kids to pick it up with their teeth while standing on one foot. After everybody does this, roll the bag down two more inches. Continue until the bag is barely off the floor, and you have the last person in the group who can do it.
14. **WALL OF FAME**: Take those extra-special moments and pictures and immortalize the group in a poster that has the best stuff of the year. If it stays up, college students who return to the scene of their junior high crimes will love remembering what happened. Kids in the current group will fight to get their picture on the wall.
15. **WORLD RECORDS**: Everybody who's anybody is listed in the *Guinness Book* someplace. Why not

your group? Pick a bizarre idea and try to set a world record. Find something that's *not* in the book and set your own record (you're guaranteed the title this way!).

16. **HOW MANY CAN STAND ON THIS?** Take any object available (a chair, a book, the Sunday school superintendent) and see how many people can stand on it without touching anything else. Kids will get more and more creative as they watch others add to the number.

17. **PARENT COFFEE**: Have an evening at someone's house where all you do is stand before the parents and answer questions about the youth program. Everyone will be so impressed at your courage that they'll rarely ask a difficult question.

18. **INCLUSIVENESS**: Make sure whenever you have a program requiring volunteer students that you have a place for everybody. Fight the school system's "cut list" that is so demoralizing for junior highers, and let them know that the Good News is for everybody who responds.

19. **PHONE MESSAGE**: Have a hot line phone number that kids can call for the message of the week. Leave wild and strange messages that make them interested in calling the church. In the middle of the message, plug your next event or your birthday party.

20. **SILK SCREENING**: Kids love cool and colorful T-shirts. Stop by an art supply store and buy the simple equipment for silk screening (including ink). Let the kids make their own designs and do their own printing; they'll do some fantastic things (like silk screening their only nice coat).

By the way, let a silk screen shop transfer the pattern to the screen—you'll go crazy trying to make it work with a heat lamp.

21. **THEMES**: Go nuts with themes. Take anything happening in the country at this moment and develop a theme out of it. As I write this, ecology is back in vogue. Build a night around it.

22. **VIDEO CLIPS**: Use short clips of video that you've filmed. Somehow, a skit that is dull live will be great on the screen. Make videos of anything kids are watching on the tube—your attempt at similarity will keep them watching.

23. **SIX-PACK ON FIRE**: Take the plastic that holds a six-pack of pop together, stretch it until you have a long piece of plastic, and hang it from a tree branch by a piece of string so that it's not touching the tree. Light the plastic (yes, it lights) and watch the weird result: Short bursts of flame will drip from the plastic. This must be done in the dark! It's a great way to get the group to focus as you play a song or read a Scripture in the background. (CAUTION: Try this beforehand to make sure you are in control of the situation. Be careful not to pick a place where something could catch on fire, and be outside where the ventilation is best. Make sure you have adequate supervision to ensure that the flame doesn't burn out of control, and tell the kids not to try this one on their own!).

24. **OVERGROWN GAMES**: Find some giant scaffolding and set it up in the room with the highest ceiling. Play *Hollywood Squares* or straight tic-tac-toe with people sitting on the

scaffolding. Make a giant "Scrabble" board. Play huge "Monopoly" or "Trivial Pursuit" (a six-foot foam die is a kick to throw from the sanctuary balcony).

25. **SHAVE FOR A LAUGH**: Promise to shave your beard if your group attendance reaches twenty-five kids by next month. Shave your head if you hit 100. Shave everybody's head if you hit 150. Do something to change your look—a complete makeover might be in order. Maybe because they're still trying to be comfortable with their own looks, junior highers love to watch adults make fun of themselves. So do it! If you're female and can't shave your beard (or don't want to because you *like* being the only woman in town with a Fu Manchu), find something about yourself that the kids can make fun of. Short, blonde, waddle when you walk (wait a minute—these are all things my students poke fun at!).

26. **CATCH THEM DOING SOMETHING RIGHT**: Every kid needs to be noticed when he or she does a small and seemingly insignificant thing. Reward them for those small steps. You might be shocked when a few years later an adult tells you that that moment shaped her or his life considerably. Wasn't it once true of you?

STEVE'S TWENTY-SIX INCREDIBLY HOT PROGRAM IDEAS AND TIPS

1. **STAY IN A HOTEL**: It's quite a privilege for junior high kids to stay in a hotel . . . without their parents! It could be fun to make an event out of simply staying in the hotel or wrapping it around another activity (dinner, shopping, amusement park, movie). You can keep costs affordable by inquiring about group discounts and sleeping four to five kids per room.

2. **CREATE YOUR OWN LOGO**: Create a logo to represent your group on stationery, business cards, T-shirts, and just about anything. It's great for group identity and promotion. Have a contest and let your kids create the logo, or you can hire a graphic artist to create it.

3. **GET ON OTHER YOUTH LEADERS' MAILING LISTS**: Pick out a few churches and ask to be put on their mailing lists so you receive the same flyers kids receive. They might want to be put on your list, too. Be sure to offer to pay for postage.

4. **PRIZE BAG**: I keep a bag in my office that's full of all sorts of wild prizes. When we have a game, a contest, or an event that could warrant a prize, I let the kids pull one out of the prize bag. The prizes are fun odds and ends that I collect (lost and found items, stuff I'm throwing out of the house, crazy things I've found lying around). The crazier, the better!

5. **GRADUATION GIFTS**: When your kids graduate from your group, give them creative gifts. You might edit together all your videos and give kids a copy of the finished product. You can also make copies of photographs and create picture books. How about giving a sharp Christian book or a

music tape? One year I gave away subscriptions to a Christian high school magazine (expensive, but a neat way of processing them into the high school scene).

6. **BICYCLE RODEO**: How about turning a parking lot into a rodeo corral and using a bicycle? You can create a series of contests and events: a sprint race, a joust using water balloons, roping a wooden sawhorse, an obstacle course, and so on.

7. **BUY A VIDEO CAMERA**: Okay, you can rent or borrow one. A video camera is one of the best investments my church has ever made. For awesome ideas, pick up the book *101 Outrageous Things to Do With a Video Camera* by Rick Bundschuh.[1] I love this little book!

8. **TAPING UP POSTERS**: Here's a little trick on taping signs and posters to a wall so you can reuse the poster. You know how the edge of a paper tears when you try to remove the tape? Place flat pieces of tape along the back edges of the sign. When you hang up the sign, roll pieces of tape and place them on the flat pieces. When you remove the sign, the rolled tape peels right off—no tears!

9. **POSTCARDS**: I like to collect postcards—especially off-the-wall ones. I make a habit of mailing them to a couple of kids each week. I also mail them to my core kids when I travel. They love it! You can pick up odd postcards from garage sales, rummage yards, and many stores. You can also purchase crazy tear-out postcards from the humorous section of many bookstores.

10. **PARENTS' PAGE**: It's smart to have a lot of communication with parents. Write a summary of your midweek program's lesson theme and make it available for parents. The page should include a brief overview of what you talked about, a few discussion questions for the kids and the parents to talk about, and some recommended reading on your topic. This page is a great way of integrating what the kids learn at church into the home. It's good PR, too.

11. **JUNIOR HIGH INFORMATION TABLE**: I believe that communication is essential to our ministries. Each Sunday morning at our church, I have a table in a key location. The table has a big "Junior High Ministries" sign and is stocked with a variety of our flyers and brochures. Occasionally we'll staff it with kids, leaders, or parents. It's a great way to communicate to the church in general that something great is going on in junior high.

12. **SPIRITUAL NOTEBOOK**: Invest in three-ring binders and give (or sell) them to your kids for keeping track of their spiritual growth. Include sections on prayer, personal Bible study, journaling, and letters to God. Also include sections for youth group member addresses, ministry flyers, songs, and notes. The goal is to have the kids bring their notebooks to church with them.

13. **CHRISTIAN MUSIC TAPE CLUB**: You can join a Christian music cassette tape club and get some of the latest releases of Christian music's best at discount prices. One group, Interl'inc, also offers Bible study guides based on the songs and a spe-

cial club just for kids. Joining the club is a great way of keeping yourself and your kids up on the latest. It's also a good way to get tapes. Contact Interl'inc at P.O. Box 21806, Waco, TX 76702.

14. **USE THE CEILING**: We fill up walls with posters and signs, so why not put them on the ceiling, too? I find that whenever I use the ceiling, it gets the kids' attention. Recently I wrote out the points of my talk on poster paper and taped them to the ceiling. I had the kids lie on their backs "reading" the ceiling while I talked to them. Whenever I use creative means to communicate truth, I usually win.

15. **STAFF BIOGRAPHIES**: Write up a brief bio on each of your volunteer staff leaders and make them available. It's a great information sheet for parents, and it shows off your incredible staff. You have sharp people working with you and any way you can highlight them is good PR.

16. **CAN YOU THROW IT?** This is a pretty odd thing my group does. For a consecutive number of weeks, we bring kids out of the group to try to throw an object for distance. We throw such things as a tissue, a tortilla, a sofa, and even cow pies (what a mess). Once we even threw a small junior higher!

17. **SHOE KICK AND RECORD TOSS**: Stuck for a last minute game and have a lot of room? Try having kids kick off their shoes for distance. Another one is to see how far you can throw an old record. Keep old records just for that purpose.

18. **PARENTS' NIGHT**: Each year (sometimes twice a year), we have a special parents' night during our midweek Toozday Night program. The trick is that we run the program just like we always run it, and the parents participate as if they were junior highers, too. It's a great way of letting the parents see what we do by doing what we do. (P.S.—they love it!)

19. **ODDBALL PHONE CALLS**: Calling kids on the phone is great contact work. Out of my need for creativity or my tendency to be a bit off center, I have started doing goofy things when I call the kids. I'll pretend I'm a radio DJ calling with the million dollar question (talk into a jar or a can for an echo), a pollster collecting information on odd trivia (do they breathe through the left or right nostril most?), or even a youth worker who likes them. The kids get a kick out of it (parents think I'm crazy) and look forward to the calls. Yes, I talk serious with them, too.

20. **JUNIOR HIGH RESOURCE LIBRARY**: Gather a group of books, magazines, videos, and music cassettes that are relevant to junior highers. Create a checkout system and let the kids use them.

21. **SAVE OLD MAGAZINES**: Save old magazines and keep a big box of them for your group. They're useful for making posters, collages, some games, and general art stuff when you cut them up. They're also great for getting ideas for talk titles. Stack about fifteen of them together and rip the bunch in two to impress your kids (yeah, right).

22. **MISSIONS PIGGY BANK**: Get a large (or giant) piggy bank (yes, a bank shaped like a pig). Have your

kids drop their Sunday offerings in a pig. Raising money for a missions project? Have a ceremony at the end of the project and have the junior highers literally break the bank.

23. **TRIVIA MANIA**: Junior highers really like to answer trivia questions (since they think they know everything anyway, this gives them the chance to prove it). Collect trivia books on all sorts of topics. They come in handy when you have time to fill or you need an emergency game. You can have fun with audio trivia ideas: Tape famous TV voices off the set, tape TV theme songs, or tape songs off the radio.

24. **BIG BUCKS**: During recreation events, I got tired of just awarding points (what are points, anyhow?), so I gave away money that I printed on our church press. Before you report me for counterfeiting, the bills have my picture in the center and are called "Big Bucks" (our kids dubbed them "Dickie Dollars"). When we play games, I have a stack in my pocket (like Monty Hall on *Let's Make a Deal*), and I hand them out as points. The kids get into it. One night (true story) I told them that a local hamburger place would give them a 15 percent discount if they paid with "Dickie Dollars." Quite a few of them tried!

25. **FOOD SERVICE BILLBOARD**: A church I know puts up a menu board in its youth room—like a menu in a hamburger joint. You've seen them—the letters are attached to the board and it usually has a soft drink slogan at the top. The group uses the board as a way of advertising upcoming events. It really looks cool.

26. **CRAZY QUESTIONS**: Looking for a way to bring your group together so it can focus on what you want to do? Here's something I do that really works: I ask kids to answer pretty crazy questions. The questions usually capture their attention. I'll often use them as a way to start off a program. Sometimes I'll use them as primers for more serious questions. Our kids love them. Here are a few that can get you started on a list of your own.

Crazy Questions List

A. Why is Captain Kangaroo called Captain Kangaroo?
B. Describe when you discovered there was no Santa Claus.
C. Who's better, Rocky or Bullwinkle?
D. What sound and face do you make when you hit your funny bone?
E. Say something significant about Teenage Mutant Ninja Turtles.
F. If Batman, Spiderman, and Wonder Woman played chess, who would win?
G. What's the weirdest thing you ever did as a kid?
H. What are the first and last things you do in a day?
I. If you had a choice between watching *I Love Lucy*, *Leave It to Beaver*, or *Star Trek* reruns, which would you choose?
J. Pronounce your full name backward.
K. Make your weirdest face.
L. Girls, if you could have lunch with Wilma Flintstone, Lois Lane, or *The Brady Bunch* mom, who would you choose? Why?
M. Boys, if you could shoot hoops with Porky Pig, Peter Pan, or Ricky

Ricardo, who would you choose? Why?

N. Who is your favorite *Gilligan's Island* character? Why?

O. Create a list of useful things that can be done with a Q-tip.

Endnotes

1. Rick Bundschuh, *101 Outrageous Things to Do With a Video Camera* (Ventura, Calif.: Gospel Light/Light Force, 1988).